Contents

List of Illustrations

Chapter 1

The Objectives of an Inventory Control System

The purpose of an inventory control system is to reduce the costs associated with maintaining an inventory. These costs fall under three main headings: the cost of holding stock, the cost of not holding stock, and the cost of the work-load caused by movements of merchandise in and out of the inventory and the corresponding movements of information.

This chapter examines these three major cost headings in some detail, in order to show the basic cost factors which will determine the techniques of inventory control described in later chapters. There are very many different factors which affect the total cost of holding an inventory, and it is difficult to consider all of these simultaneously. Thus this first chapter will show what costs are involved, and subsequent chapters will describe techniques for dealing with each cost area taken separately; the final section of the book will attempt to show the interaction between each area. All the techniques described, some of them quite complex and at first sight over-sophisticated, will be aimed at reducing the total cost of inventory. They will all be related to the basic cost elements described below.

The major reason for keeping stocks of an item is to ensure that a supply of that item will be available when it is needed. The major disadvantages of keeping stocks of an item are as follows. Firstly, the goods in question have been bought or manufactured or obtained in some way which has caused the company holding these goods to pay out money. The stock has generally not been sold, so that the company has paid out money for the goods and has not yet received any compensation. It is likely that goods stored in an inventory will eventually be sold, so that any particular piece of merchandise will stay in storage for a limited time only.

Even so, when merchandise is being continuously bought into and sold from stock, there will always be a certain amount which has been paid for and is still awaiting sale, and this represents an investment of money which is providing no apparent return. The average value of the merchandise in stock represents a continuous investment of money, and this 'unproductive' investment is one of the major costs of holding inventory.

If it were possible to reduce the average value of stock held, then money would be released from inventory for use by the company, which could invest it in some other area of its activities. Suppose that a company could release £x from inventory by reducing its average inventory value from £I to £(I − x), and that the profit that a company makes from money invested in its own activities is r per cent per annum (this is likely to be a fairly high percentage – certainly higher than the Bank Rate if the company is profitable). Then the benefit to that company from this reduction in stock level is £rx per annum. If this saving is not made, the company has effectively forfeited £rx per annum in profit by keeping the £x invested in inventory. This principle is generally extended to the total inventory value, so that the cost of the total stock holding of the company is £rI per annum – which is the profit that could be made if that money invested in stock were available for use elsewhere.

An alternative method of lowering the cost of holding stock is to reduce the cost per unit of holding inventory, which will reduce the total cost though the inventory level remains the same. The different factors which contribute to the cost can be reduced once their existence is recognized; however, in most cases the major savings stem from a reduction in inventory levels, and procedures to accomplish this will be given the greatest emphasis in this book.

There are some exceptional cases where the cost of holding inventory is less clear-cut. Sometimes an organization will hold stock which is not paid for until it is sold. Under these circumstances the supplier of the stock is bearing the cost of inventory investment on behalf of the organization holding the inventory, and this cost has to be reflected in the increased price of the item to the stockholder or in lower profit margins to the supplier. In this way, the extra cost of holding stock still affects the company concerned, although it is hidden in the price of the article. This situation applies even more strongly in the case where a company forces its suppliers to maintain large stocks of merchandise at the suppliers' own premises, to be collected and paid for as required. The costs of investment and maintenance will again be reflected in the price of the merchandise.

One grave disadvantage of the situation where one company holds stock at another's expense is that the incentive to cut stock levels can be entirely lost, so that the total operation becomes irredeemably inefficient. For example, if a supplier provides merchandise to many customers on the basis that they will pay for it when and if it is resold, then there is no incentive for the individual customer to cut stocks. The supplier is bearing the major part of the cost of stock, and if an individual customer cuts his stock holding for greater efficiency, this need never be reflected in a lower price to him; he merely allows the other companies holding this merchandise more elbow room for holding unnecessarily high stocks. Likewise, where a manufacturer supplies many companies who hold stock on his own premises, he will normally charge a standard price for his product, which includes the cost of the average amount of stock he is forced to hold for all customers. Under these circumstances, whichever company holds low stocks at the manufacturer's premises relative to the volume of purchases made, is subsidizing the companies who hold larger relative stocks. In this case special discounts would have to be negotiated for holding lower stocks before it could become worth while for any individual customer to reduce the amount of stock held on his behalf.

In general, then, a company will pay for the stock it holds directly, and the cost of holding inventory will include the cost of capital tied up in stock. In some cases the cost of stock may be indirect, and special measures may have to be taken in order to provide an incentive to reduce stocks, so that the benefit obtained by doing so is credited to the correct place.

Although in most cases the cost of investment is the major cost of holding stock, there are a number of other costs, whose relative importance varies quite widely according to the individual situation.

There is an insurance cost attached to holding stock, and the amount of insurance paid will normally depend upon the degree of fire risk involved for the particular merchandise being stored. For any given type of merchandise, this amount will be proportional to the average value of stock held. The insurance cost is another cost of holding stock which can be expressed as a certain percentage per annum of the average value of stock held.

Thirdly, there is a cost of storage space attached to holding stocks of merchandise. It is more difficult to think of this cost as being directly proportional to the average value of inventory, because many expensive items are physically quite small and many cheap items relatively bulky. It may be necessary to take specific account of this variation in an inventory control system, but it is generally very convenient to be able to express the cost of inventory as a percentage of the actual value of the stock; these variations in size and price of items are therefore often ignored, and the cost of storage space considered to be proportional to the average inventory value. It must be remembered that this is an approximation, as ridiculous situations can occur when there is a wide variation in size of merchandise and when storage-space costs are high – the storage area can be overwhelmed with large amounts of cheap bulky items if it is assumed that the cost of space is always proportional to stock value. However, storage costs are generally sufficiently small to make an assumption of proportional costs quite safe.

The analysis of storage-space costs is further complicated by the fact that existing warehouse facilities will be more or less adequate for present stock levels, and that the cost of warehouse staff will be affected by the amount of inventory held, although the major consideration is the number and size of deliveries into and out of the warehouse. However, if space in a warehouse is made free by reduction of inventory levels, this space can be used for new product lines, expansion of business or other purposes. If stock is held not in a warehouse but in a working area of a factory or in the 'back room' of a retail shop, then inventory reduction will have a high payoff in terms of extra production area or extra selling and display area. The cost of space is particularly significant in a retailing operation, where rentals are relatively high.

Allied to the cost of space and warehouse facilities is the cost of stock maintenance – painting to counteract rusting, deep-freezes, humidity- and temperature-controlled environments, and so on.

Fourthly, the cost of obsolescence is a factor which varies very widely among different types of merchandise. With some items one can be reasonably sure that whatever level of stock is held it can eventually be sold. With other items there is a definite risk that some technological innovation or change in consumer demand will make the inventory unsaleable, so that it has to be written off. This problem is particularly acute in the case of women's fashion clothing, where it is the major cost of stock. In this situation, when the advantage of being able to supply goods when required is balanced against the inventory carrying cost, the optimum point comes at a very low stock level, so that extremely small stocks must be held because of the high risk of obsolescence.

A cost similar to the cost of obsolescence is that of deterioration. Some merchandise will deteriorate if it is stored for too long a period. Obvious examples where this cost is significant are all kinds of food, photographic supplies, pharmaceutical products, etc. Some kind of age control is required for this kind of merchandise in order to make sure that the first batch received is the first to be sent out; but any kind of age-control system will break down occasionally or be overwhelmed by the effect of a drop in demand, so that sometimes merchandise will be kept for too long and have to be written off. When large stocks of this type of merchandise are held, there is always a chance of a temporary drop in the sales rate; consequently the rate at which existing stocks are sold off will be reduced, and there is a danger that they may pass the age-limit. This risk can generally be assessed and costed out. For any one item the risk value will not be directly proportional to the average inventory level; it will increase more and more steeply the higher the average stock level becomes.

Other costs can also contribute to the total stock-holding cost. The cost of pilferage is an interesting example, where the cost of stock actually lost in this way must be balanced against the cost of the security procedures to counteract it. Many companies seek to minimize or control this cost by offering special prices or privileges with respect to the stock held. Food manufacturers often allow their staff to remove as much of the product as they can carry away inside themselves, for example. The cost of low-price or free sales to employees can be balanced against its tendency to inhibit pilferage. In department stores the problem is very different in that the general public is more likely to cause high pilferage costs than the staff, and extreme measures are being taken to solve this problem: closed-circuit television is becoming very popular as a method of discouraging shop-lifters. An interesting side-effect of pilferage is that the cost can be more than the mere value of the lost stock. Firstly, when pilferage occurs, the stock level of the item involved is reduced, and the likelihood of an out-of-stock situation increased, so that an extra safety margin of stock has to be held to allow for variations in both legitimate and illicit demand; unfortunately one has to provide the same level of service to both customers and shoplifters. Secondly, pilferage will often upset the stock-recording system, so that discrepancies occur between the physical stock and the stock records – it is unusual for pilferers to have the courtesy to notify the organization that a theft has occurred, so that the stock can be replenished accordingly.

These, then, are the major factors which go to make up the cost of holding stock. This cost must, however, be balanced against the advantages obtained. As stated previously, the advantage of holding inventory is that it ensures that the items stocked are available immediately when they are needed.

What is the value of having an item available when it is needed? What makes it worth while for a company to incur the cost described above and hold stocks of merchandise? There are two main answers to this question, one of which is based on the item price, the other on the convenience of having merchandise available.

If an item varies widely in price, it is advantageous to buy it when the price is low. The decision to buy stocks of such an item depends upon a forecast of its future price. If it is expected that the future price of the item will be high, and that the future demand for the item will also be sufficiently high, then it will be worth while incurring the cost of holding an inventory of the item and selling it at a later stage at a higher price than the purchase price. Once the stock-holding cost is known, and a fairly reliable forecast of future prices and future demand is obtained, then it becomes an exercise in cost accounting to decide whether it is profitable to buy the item and how much to buy. The major difficulty in this situation is to make a forecast of future prices. This kind of operation is more common where prices fluctuate seasonally, as in the case of many agricultural products. The forecasting of prices and demand in these circumstances requires considerable knowledge, skill and experience, and mathematical techniques can generally provide no more than a very rough guide for this type of operation.

The situation where mathematical techniques can be successfully applied is where the purpose of holding stock is the convenience of having it available when required. This book is mainly directed towards this situation, where the element of price which contributes to the profitability of the stock-holding operation is the difference between buying bulk quantities of merchandise at a discount and selling them at a higher price, or where the price for obtaining the merchandise is relatively constant.

In this situation, what value can be placed on having merchandise available when it is required? It will vary widely under different circumstances, as described below. In order to compare these different circumstances it is more convenient to reverse the question and to decide upon the cost of not having the item available. This cost can then be compared directly with the cost of holding the necessary stock.

The cost of not holding stock will depend upon the 'logical distance' between the inventory in question and the ultimate user of the products held in this inventory. This is not the physical distance between the two, but the number of intermediate buffer inventories between them. For example, a manufacturer may sell goods to a major wholesaler who sells to a group of retail stores who have their own central warehouse, so that there are many intermediate stages between the consumer who buys the goods at the retail outlet and the manufacturer who ultimately supplies the product.

The importance of always having a readily available supply diminishes as the distance from the ultimate consumer increases. When a customer arrives at a retail shop in order to buy a certain item, it is extremely important that a stock of that item be available. In broad terms, the result of being out of stock at the retail level is lost sales: the customer will generally go elsewhere for his requirements. There are several factors which modify the direct relationship between out-of-stock situations and lost sales, but usually the major effect of stock-outs in retail is lost sales. If a retailer holds low stocks of an item, so that it is out of stock for, say, ten days per year on average, then the annual cost of not holding larger stocks is the profit that would have been made from ten days' sales of that item. It is often convenient to think of the stock level of an item in terms of the number and seriousness of out-of-stock situations it is likely to produce. The measure of stock effectiveness normally used for this kind of evaluation is the 'service level'. This is defined as the item sales divided by the item demand. Thus, in the case quoted above, assuming that the item in question sold at a steady rate day by day, the annual sales of the item would be 254 days' sales during the year. The retailer in the example lost 10 days' sales, so that the resultant service level would be 244/254, or approximately 96 per cent. (The level of service is normally expressed as a percentage.)

A.I.C.T.—2

If a retail inventory is maintained at a level which will provide a 96 per cent level of service, the retailer is accepting a loss of 4 per cent of his potential profit. This should of course cost him less than the extra stock-holding cost necessary to capture that extra demand if he is operating at the correct service level. This view of the level of service in retail is, however, over-simplified. There are several factors which modify the assumption that a stock-out means lost sales.

If a retailer's overall service level is significantly lower than that provided by his local competitors, he will have more frequent stock-outs and his customers will become dissatisfied and tend to patronize shops which provide a higher level of service (all other things being equal). Thus the costs of not holding stock can be rather more than the theoretical lost sales figure. On the other hand, several factors work in the retailer's favour, so that the cost of a stock-out is not always lost sales. In some cases the customer will defer his purchase until the stock becomes available. This is not very usual, but will occur with some types of merchandise, and will mean that the retailer in fact loses fewer sales than one would theoretically expect. A second, very significant, factor which minimizes the actual lost sales is the substitutability factor. In many cases, although the customer has come to buy a particular article, he may be willing to accept another, similar article if the original is not available. If a retailer stocks both Heinz and Crosse & Blackwell baked beans, he might hold stocks which would provide a 90 per cent level of service on each brand separately. Let us assume for the sake of argument that 50 per cent of the customers intending to buy one brand would be willing to buy the other if their usual choice is out of stock. That is, we define a 'substitutability factor' of 50 per cent between Heinz and Crosse & Blackwell baked beans. The effective service level over the two brands would then be greater than 90 per cent, even though the individual service levels on each item separately are only 90 per cent. The chances of both brands being out of stock simultaneously are only about 1 per cent, so that 1 per cent of sales will be lost in any event. In the remaining 9 per cent of cases, where one will be in stock while the other is out of stock, 50 per cent of the customers will be willing to accept a substitute, giving a resultant lost sales percentage of $4\frac{1}{2}$ per cent, plus the 1 per cent where both were out of stock simultaneously. Thus the service level provided will be not 90 but $94\frac{1}{2}$ per cent over the two brands. Normally the importance of substitution in retail is minimized, because it is so difficult to define. Very few retailers feel able to state precisely what degree of substitutability exists between the various items in their merchandise range.

Moving one step further away from the ultimate consumer, at the local warehouse level the penalty for being understocked is apparently much less. The local warehouse will accept orders from retailers, and will occasionally be out of stock. When this happens, lost sales may result. However, the retailer is accustomed to a delay between making an order and receiving the merchandise requested. This delay, the time elapsing between deciding to make an order and having the merchandise available for use, is generally called the 'lead time' of the merchandise. There are three components of this lead time. Firstly, there is the time to recognize that an order should be placed. Unless the stock is under continuous review, and orders can be placed immediately a shipment or sale has been made, there is generally a lag between the need for stock replenishment and the realization that a new order should be placed. This should occur the next time the stock of the item in question is reviewed. Secondly, there is the time between the placing of the order and its receipt – which will depend on the clerical procedures, stock position and delivery methods of the supplier. This factor tends to be variable and outside the control of the customer. Thirdly, there is the time taken to inspect the delivery, move it to the storage area and report the receipt to the stock records. The first and third of these factors can be reduced by efficient control procedures, and can result in some reduction of inventory levels. If the warehouse is out of stock, but expects a delivery in the near future, it will not matter very much if the lead time is increased by a few days. The retailer is accustomed to variations in lead time caused by postal delays, scheduling problems at the warehouse loading bay, the exact configuration of delivery routes, variations in work-load in the clerical procedures, passing the order through to the warehouse area, picking and assembling the order, and so on. Even when the wholesaler is out of stock, and not expecting a delivery for some time, the retailer will generally have some stock left, and may be able to accept a longer lead time until the merchandise arrives at the warehouse without being forced out of stock himself.

Orders from retailer to wholesaler involve much larger quantities than the amount required by an individual customer at the retail shop. The warehouse may be able to ration out its stock, supplying a proportion of the total amount ordered for immediate use, and sending on the balance when new supplies arrive. The wholesaler can fill orders partially in two ways: he may supply merchandise for only some of the lines on an order form, or he may send partial quantities of those lines he can supply.

Although the wholesaler is less likely to lose sales directly through stock-outs, there are significant costs associated with a low level of service at the warehouse. These are generally more difficult to isolate and quantify than in the retail situation.

Before these costs are discussed, a slight modification is required to the definition of 'level of service' to make it applicable to both retail and wholesale. It must be redefined as *the sales of an item made immediately from stock, divided by the item demand.*

It is worth noting that while the effect of stock-outs in retail is easier to estimate, it is far more difficult to assess what service level is in fact being provided; although sales are known or easily calculated, it is very difficult to calculate the demand. Attempts have been made to carry out sampling studies, or to ask customers whether they obtained all they required, but the results are somewhat doubtful. Some retailers have asked their sales clerks to make a record of all items requested that were not in stock, but this generally founders because the sales clerk does not do this reliably and because customers often do not ask for merchandise; if it is not displayed they assume that it is not available.

The wholesaler, however, generally has a hard copy of all orders. Even if orders are made by telephone the clerk will write them down, and it is relatively easy to ascertain what proportion of the total value of merchandise ordered is dispatched immediately from stock.

The costs of not holding stock at the wholesale level are mainly associated with administrative inconvenience and customer satisfaction. When a stock-out occurs, it is impossible to supply the order immediately. The order will have to wait in a pending or 'back-order' file until the merchandise arrives in stock again. This entails constant checking of the back-order file to detect the arrival of stock which is to be dispatched immediately, which involves considerable clerical labour.

It is not usual to delay the entire delivery because some lines in the order cannot be supplied. Therefore part of the order will be sent and part placed in the back-order file. This entails two or more sets of delivery notes, invoicing procedures, and physical deliveries for each order which contains a line that is out of stock. Action may have to be taken to expedite delivery from the warehouse's supplier if the stock-out is particularly serious. This again takes up considerable administrative time and effort. In total, the above considerations amount to a very heavy clerical work-load and correspondingly heavy costs if the service level is low.

The second major factor to be considered in wholesale is customer satisfaction. If a wholesaler is frequently out of stock, his lead time to the retailer will become more erratic, because he is often unable to supply immediately. If the retailer is to keep a good in-stock position, he must allow for the maximum likely delay in supplying his order. If he sells 10 per day of a particular item, and the normal lead time is five days, he will reorder the item when he has about 50 in stock. However, if the lead time may be anything between five and ten days, he must allow for the worst possibility, and reorder when he has 100 units in stock. Because the lead time is erratic, very often the delivery will arrive after only five days, so that the retailer finds himself with 50 more items in stock than he planned. If the wholesaler provides an erratic lead time to the retailer, he causes him to hold more stock than necessary. By allowing his stock level (and hence his level of service) to drop, the wholesaler is forcing the retailer to hold larger stocks in order to maintain his own stock position. The wholesaler is passing on the responsibility for holding stock to the retailer. If this situation is allowed to get very bad, the retailer will take his custom elsewhere; in extreme cases he may decide to order directly from the manufacturer. After a certain point is passed it is better to have a long, reliable lead time than a short, erratic lead time. In other words, if a wholesaler allows his service level to drop below a certain point, he is opting out of his major function, which is to provide a convenient local supply of merchandise at fairly short notice, and his business will suffer in proportion.

Certain other, less important, costs are incurred by a low level of service in wholesaling. Orders often have to be split so that available lines are sent at once and out-of-stock lines deferred; consequently transportation occurs more frequently, perhaps with uneconomically small loads, or larger numbers of drops per journey. The retailer may be ordering a quantity which is economical for his own purposes; if the wholesaler often sends partial quantities this will entail an extra load on the retailer's receiving and marking department and upset his normal ordering and receiving cycle.

Moving from the wholesale level, several stages further away from the consumer, similar arguments apply to the major wholesaler and to the manufacturer who holds stocks of finished products. There are more buffer stocks in between the inventory point and the eventual demand, so that delays in supply can be passed down the distribution network, and at each level the individual inventories may be able to take up some of the slack. The longer the chain of supply, the less pressure is exerted to maintain a high level of service, quantities become greater, partial delivery more acceptable, and so on. Nevertheless, the considerations of administrative inconvenience and customer dissatisfaction still apply to manufacturers and major wholesalers. Furthermore, there are several special effects and objectives applicable to these organizations which make it very difficult to maintain correct stock levels, as will be discussed later.

Having shown the major factors which affect stock-holding costs and stock-out costs at various levels of inventory relative to the consumer, the next step is to examine the various ways in which these factors apply to different types of industry in retailing, wholesaling and manufacturing respectively.

Chapter 2

The Variations in Inventory Objectives and Environment Across Different Industries

Although it is relatively more important to maintain a high level of service in a retail environment, it is significant that retailers generally hold a much wider range of items than wholesalers; furthermore, they hold this wide range of items in a large number of separate locations. This means that the magnitude of the retailer's problem is much greater in terms of the sheer number of different items which have to be controlled. Likewise, wholesalers generally hold a wider range of goods than manufacturers, often in several regional depots. This means that retailers usually provide relatively low service levels, and manufacturers high service levels. It is difficult to quote definite figures, but as a guide to the kind of difference which does exist between these operations, representative figures might be as follows: retail average service level 85 per cent, wholesale 94 per cent, and manufacturers 99 per cent. This is, of course, in direct opposition to the importance of maintaining high service in these respective areas. The financial effects of stock-holding costs also vary widely over the different levels of distribution.

When a manager looks at his company accounts, there will be one column which he will regard as a necessary evil. This is the column of figures showing the value of inventory held by the company. Managers resent having large amounts of money frozen in the form of goods and materials which are apparently serving no useful purpose. This is true even when the main reason for the company's existence is to hold stock, as is the case in wholesale and retail companies. They feel that the amount of money invested in inventory is out of all proportion to the usefulness of the inventory; however, they see no way of reducing the levels in practice without taking considerable risks or instituting very expensive methods of stock control. In the U.K. approximate levels of investment in inventory are as follows. The total stock holding of retailers is about £1,500 million, and wholesalers hold about £1,000 million worth of merchandise. Quite a large proportion of manufactured goods, particularly expensive capital equipment, does not pass through the wholesale or retail level, so that the figures for all manufacturing companies in the country are rather higher. The amount of money tied up in the form of finished products at the manufacturer's premises is about £1,500 million, as semi-processed parts or products in the process of being made the total investment is £2,000 million, and the total stocks of raw materials and fuel amount to another £2,000 million.

It can be seen that the problem of inventory investment is common to all levels of industry, although the emphasis on each facet of the problem varies according to the industry and type of product. There are five convenient divisions into which most inventories can be classified. These are: raw materials and fuel being held to supply a production process; semi-processed goods being held during the production cycle, whose 'value' increases with every operation that is performed on them; stocks of finished goods waiting to be sold at the manufacturing location; stocks in regional depots or warehouses; and finally stocks held in a retail outlet. As shown by the above investment figures, the amount of capital tied up at each of these levels is of the same order of magnitude.

The first major cost factor discussed in Chapter 1 – the cost of holding stock – varies quite widely over different industries. A viable company should obtain a percentage return from investing in its own operations which is well above the Bank Rate. Added to this 'opportunity cost' of the capital tied up in inventory are the extra cost elements described in Chapter 1. It is difficult to quote a generally applicable average figure for stock-holding costs, but 25 per cent per annum is a not unreasonable estimate. The relative importance of the individual components of the carrying cost also differ according to industry and type of product. The cost of capital should be between 8 and 15 per cent, depending upon the need for capital, profit per pound invested, and the company's liquidity. The cost of obsolescence may be anything from zero (in the case of most food products) to 30 per cent (in the case of women's fashions). Insurance will apply at different rates for lumber yards, petroleum and metal ingots, for example. It should be between 0·2 and 4 per cent per annum. Storage-space costs are generally less than 5 per cent per annum of the average inventory value. This will vary according to the bulk of the item and whether special equipment is needed to maintain it in good condition. Some countries provide another incentive to cut inventory in that taxes are levied on company assets. In this situation, tax is paid in proportion to the average value of inventory held, which is a direct cost to be added to the inventory carrying cost. Because it is made up of a number of very variable factors, the total cost of carrying inventory has a wide possible range: it may be anything between 8 per cent and 60 per cent per annum in any individual case.

In a retail operation, the major cost factors are the cost of not holding stock and the cost of obsolescence (for fashion merchandise). The cost of not holding stock is at its highest in retail, as it is here that stock-outs are most likely to produce lost sales. If a retail store customer cannot be supplied with the merchandise he requires directly from stock, then he will go elsewhere, and the retailer will have lost the profit he would have made from making the sale.

Another cost of not holding stock which is difficult to quantify is the cost of customer dissatisfaction caused by failure to provide the merchandise requested. The supermarket concept of shopping is gaining ground quite rapidly. People are becoming more used to buying as many items as possible at one single location, and they dislike having to go elsewhere for merchandise which is out of stock at the first location they visit. This means that there will be a tendency to visit the shop with the best in-stock position first, in the hope of being able to make all the planned purchases at one location. If the customer is very often frustrated in this purpose, and has to go elsewhere to complete his or her purchases, the chances are quite high that some other retailer will consistently supply the gaps in the range, and the customer will tend to visit him first rather than the previous first choice. Consistent out-of-stock situations can cause a retailer to lose his customers in the long term, as well as losing him individual sales in the short term.

The cost of holding stock at the retail level is unusually high in the case of fashion merchandise. Women's clothing in particular has a very high obsolescence rate, and the selling life of a style of dress or shoe may be less than ten weeks. This means that very low inventory levels must be kept, otherwise the cost of holding stock (including a large obsolescence factor) far outweighs the profit made from selling merchandise. This is one of the reasons why such high mark-ups are charged for very fashionable merchandise. It is not unknown for selling prices to be more than double the cost price, although it is more common for them to be about 70 per cent up on cost. The obsolescence problem is much less acute with more staple merchandise, and mark-ups are generally lower.

The cost of storage space is much higher in retail than in other areas. This is because retail stores are usually in areas where the cost of renting space is high, such as the centres of towns and cities. Warehouses and manufacturing plants are normally in much lower-cost areas. The retailer also has the problem that he generally sells only merchandise which is on display in his selling area. However, the density of storage must be much lower in this area, so that the customers can see all the merchandise and can circulate. The retailer needs a back-room store where merchandise can be piled up for concentrated storage, and from which the display areas can be replenished. The larger the back-room store, the more space is taken away from the selling area, so that the cost of bulk storage to the retailer is quite high. Insurance costs to a retailer are also high, because of the large number of people passing through the store. Fire risks can be reduced by imposing a no-smoking rule in the store, but this can cause some customer resentment.

Certain types of retailer avoid these problems to some extent. Mail-order organizations, for example, can site themselves in relatively low-cost areas, and have some leeway in supplying items directly from stock. Nevertheless, such companies generally place great emphasis on speed of supply for the orders placed by their agents or customers, and take great pains to be in stock. They like to be able to supply rapidly because of the danger that an agent may lose interest or move to another mail-order company.

At the regional depot or wholesale level of distribution, the importance of being in stock is slightly less. If the warehouse provides a low level of service, the burden of stock holding is passed on to the retailer. This is generally inefficient, because the increase in stock held by all the retailers who buy from this warehouse will be greater than the amount of stock saved by the warehouse in dropping to a lower service level. If the regional depot is part of the same organization as the retail outlets, then the total stock holding of the organization will be larger if the depot holds inadequate stock levels. If the depot is an independent wholesale operation, then its customers will become dissatisfied and begin to patronize other wholesalers or to order from the manufacturer.

Apart from the long-term customer satisfaction problem, some retailers will cancel the immediate order and go elsewhere if a rapid delivery is not assured, so that some percentage of the back-orders will be directly lost sales. This proportion is generally between 20 and 80 per cent. Another cost attached to back-orders is the special treatment they must receive, the necessity to ask for urgent deliveries of out-of-stock items and to process these rapidly; there is always some extra clerical cost when a back-order occurs. Costs of holding stock at the wholesale level are high, and often constitute the largest single annual cost to the wholesaler.

The objectives of stock management for finished-goods inventories at the manufacturing location depend upon whether the manufacturer's customers are wholesalers, retailers or the ultimate consumer or client, and upon the type of production process involved.

If the demand for an item is a direct demand from the consumer, it will be subject to large fluctuations. If orders are passed through a chain of retail and wholesale stock-holding locations, then large random fluctuations and violent seasonal peaks in demand will be smoothed out, so that the demand peaks reach lower levels and are spread over longer periods. If, for example, a product has a very sharp peak in sales during December — assuming that it is an item which sells very well immediately before Christmas — then, because of the different lead times and buffer stock situations at retail and wholesale level, the peak may well be smoothed out to a lower-level surge in demand during October and November by the time the orders reach the manufacturer, as different wholesalers and retailers plan ahead at differing intervals of time.

A long distribution chain or network of this kind has its own peculiar disadvantages, and the benefits of the smoother pattern of demand are counterbalanced by the unusual effects which can occur. Such a network is likely to set up internal oscillations in demand. This process has been analysed in detail by Forrester, and an exposition of some of his conclusions can be found in his book *Industrial Dynamics* (see Bibliography).

The effects described by Forrester can be demonstrated quite simply in the following fashion. Take four people, and assign them to be a retailer, a local wholesaler, a national wholesaler and a manufacturer respectively. Give each one 20 counters to represent his stock of a particular item, and assign a simple stock-control rule that each man should aim to keep an average stock of 20 counters. Put orders of 4 items in the pipeline between each level, and demand 4 items from the retailer for a few time-periods so that 4 is established as the average demand throughout the network. Then increase the demand on the retailer to 6 per period. His basic stock is 20. He will sell 6, and receive his previous order of 4, leaving him a stock of 18. He will therefore plan to have 6 more ordered for the next period's supply, plus 2 more to bring his stock up to 20. The retailer will then order 8 units from the wholesaler. The local wholesaler, not knowing the retail demand, will have received his normal supply of 4, and will have sold 8, so that his remaining stock will be 16. He will order 8 to satisfy next month's demand, and 4 more to bring his stock up to 20. This means that an order of 12 is placed on the national wholesaler, who will end up with 12 in stock. He in turn will order 12 for next period's demand, plus 8 to bring his stock up to 20. Thus an order of 20 units is placed on the manufacturer, who will make 40 units for stock. When the next series of demands comes through, each level will attempt to compensate by ordering less, and oscillations will be set up in the system. The actual figures which might result from carrying out this simple simulation exercise are shown below.

Retail Demand	Stock	Local Demand	Stock	National Demand	Stock	Manufacturer Demand	Stock	Made
4	20	4	20	4	20	4	20	4
	16		16		16		16	
4	20	4	20	4	20	4	20	4
	16		16		16		16	
6	20	4	20	4	20	4	20	4
	14		16		16		16	
6	18	8	20	4	20	4	20	4
	12		12		16		16	
6	20	6	16	12	20	4	20	4
	14		10		8		16	
6	20	6	22	5	12	20	20	4
	14		16		7		0	
6	20	6	21	5	27	3	4	40
	14		15		22		1	
6	20	6	20	6	25	1	41	0
	14		14		19		40	
6	20	6	20	6	20	6	40	0
	14		14		14		34	
6	20	6	20	6	20	6	34	0
	14		14		14		28	
6	20	6	20	6	20	6	28	0
	14		14		14		22	
6	20	6	20	6	20	6	22	4

In this example the lead times are consistent and short, and the stock controller is assumed to be reacting very quickly to the changes in demand level. This will not necessarily be the case in practice. The demand figures used are extremely stable, with a slight upsurge. The effect of the small variation in level of sales at the retail location has caused giant fluctuations in the stock level of the manufacturer's finished-product warehouse, and has disrupted the even flow of his production process.

In a real situation, where random fluctuations, changes in demand level, and acute seasonal peaks occur at the retail end of the system, each causing their own complex series of oscillations and harmonics superimposed upon one another, the shape of demand to the manufacturer's finished-goods inventory and production processes is an insane combination of real and artificial cyclical processes, which may combine or cancel each other out, and are continuously dampening out and regenerating themselves.

Most manufacturers in this situation try to obtain information on what is actually happening at the retail level, so that some guidance in deciding whether demand changes are real or artificial can be obtained. For example, the major purpose of offering guarantee cards to be filled in is usually to obtain an estimate of retail demand levels. It is assumed that a fairly consistent percentage of customers will fill in and return guarantee cards, so that any change in level in the number of cards returned provides an indication of a proportionate variation in the level of retail demand, giving early warning of future changes. This problem cannot be significantly improved by changing the stock-control system at each individual level; the only solution is to collect information as to what is happening at the lower levels, and use this for planning purposes.

Where there is a seasonal demand for a product, there will be a predictable yearly cycle of orders, with random variations and artificial oscillations superimposed. If the manufacturer produces the finished goods by a production-line process, he will want to keep his rate of production fairly constant, for optimum machine utilization. Therefore one of the major purposes of his finished-goods inventory will be to smooth out the demand on production.

These two objectives, the maintenance of low stock levels and of steady production, must be balanced against each other in the production of finished-goods inventories.

During a high selling season, or a peak in orders, whether this peak is a random fluctuation, a normal seasonal upswing or an artificial oscillation, the production line will be making less than the demand, and the difference will be made up from inventory. During a period of low demand, the production line will produce more than the demand, and excess production will go into the warehouse. Ideally, any changes in production capacity will be in the form of long-term expansion of production facilities and the ability to vary the amount of overtime worked in cases of emergency.

If the production process is not continuous, the stock levels held will depend to a great extent on the cost of producing a batch of the product. If it is very costly to switch the production line or to set up the necessary machines for a run of the item concerned, then it will be of advantage to produce large batches for inventory, and to make this last as long as possible until a new set-up and production cycle is required. Under these conditions, the inventory can be used to batch the demand into large short-term demands rather than to smooth the production rate.

The value of merchandise being processed at any one time will depend upon the length of the production process and the scheduling rules used to assign production priorities. If the rule is made that any batch that has been started must be completed as soon as possible — that is, the more work that has been done on it, the higher the priority — then the value of in-process inventory will be minimized, but a penalty will be paid in that urgently required batches may be delayed. This is another of the 'trade-off' situations in inventory control where one cost must be balanced against another.

Raw-material inventories are generally kept at a high level. The cost of holding stock is still quite high, but the number of locations involved is usually small. The penalty for being out of stock of raw materials is normally very high, as this will often disrupt the production process and may cause out-of-stock situations right down the distribution network.

It is generally felt that raw materials should be kept at very high stock levels so as not to spoil the ship for a ha'porth of tar. The value added to the product by the manufacturing and marketing process is usually large compared with the raw-material cost, so that the safety of the production process normally has much higher priority than the desire to keep low stock levels of raw materials.

The supply of raw materials is often erratic and subject to large seasonal and random fluctuations, especially in the case of agricultural produce. Raw materials are often imported or have long delivery times, and hence are subject to variations in transportation time and availability. For these reasons, either the buying strategy or the production requirements take precedence over the cost of holding stock, and raw-material inventories build up to high levels.

Chapter 3
The Setting of Safety Stocks

In the inventory management environment discussed in Chapters 1 and 2, one common thread passes through all the different stock situations: there is always a considerable cost involved in holding stocks, and this must be balanced against the penalties incurred for being out of stock. Generally the amount of stock held can be thought of as providing a certain level of service; this service level is a measure of the frequency and seriousness of stock-outs, that is, how long the stock-outs last and their consequent effect on the demand for the item. In order to decide the balance that should be maintained between stock investment and level of service, many factors must be considered, and a discussion of this question is deferred until a later chapter. Before deciding what the balance between stock holding and stock-outs should be, it is necessary to examine stock levels and service levels more closely, and to be able to control service levels in order to produce the desired balance. This chapter examines some of the simpler interactions between stock level and service level, and some of the methods which can be used to control these interactions.

Whatever service level is decided upon as being the 'best' level for a particular inventory, it is desirable to achieve that level for a minimum stock cost. An inventory is made up of many different items, each of which may have a different average stock holding and service level. In order to achieve a given overall service level for the inventory, it is necessary to control the individual service levels of the items comprising the inventory. If this is done by investing money in the stock of different items in the correct proportions – so as to produce, for example, one identical service level for all items – then the overall service level objective will have been achieved for the minimum cost of stock holding.

It is difficult to control the output from an inventory control system; the demands made upon stock are out of the control of the company holding the inventory, and the major problem is to decide when to replenish the inventory. In a manufacturing environment, demand is sometimes known very accurately for a short period in advance, but by then these are firm orders, and it may be too late to plan for the load involved. Generally there is considerable difficulty in predicting sales far enough ahead to be able to control stock perfectly. It is relatively easy to obtain more stock, but difficult to control the sales rate from stock, so that the emphasis in stock control is placed on controlling the orders for more merchandise.

One major exception to this principle is the case of retail fashion goods, where it is often difficult to obtain further supplies of an item, and great emphasis is placed on controlling the sales through price changes, promotions, prominent display, mark-downs and clearance sales. But in general, stock control boils down to order control. Factors affecting the inventory level are sales, receipts, previous stocks, and occasional adjustments, according to the formula:

new balance = old balance − sales + receipts ± adjustments.

These factors are mostly out of the control of the company holding the inventory, although sales can be controlled (to become zero) by allowing stock to run out completely. The only factor in the equation which can easily be controlled is the receipts, which can be controlled by means of orders.

Consider the process of placing orders for more merchandise from the point of view of the stock controller. He must plan well in advance when placing orders, because there will be a certain lead time which must elapse between the moment of decision and the arrival of the merchandise. Therefore orders for a new supply of merchandise must generally be placed when there is still enough stock available to last out for the lead time. The stock controller will rarely know exactly what the demand is going to be during the lead time, so he will have to make some estimate of the expected demand. This estimate will turn out to be more or less accurate in the event, depending on the skill of the stock controller and whether any unusual variations in demand occur during the lead-time period.

The penalty for being out of stock is usually higher than the penalty for carrying excessively high stocks, so that the stock controller will usually ensure that he places an order while there is still enough stock to satisfy the *maximum likely demand* during the lead time. Lead times vary, as well as demand rates, so that he will probably have to cater for the maximum likely demand during the maximum likely lead time.

It is worth while at this stage to analyse more precisely what is meant by 'the maximum likely demand'; in particular, just how 'likely' is the maximum allowable demand? It is convenient to think of this likelihood in terms of a percentage probability. In order to be able to cover the maximum *possible* demand, the controller will have to hold almost infinite stock levels. There must therefore be some cut-off decision as to the level at which it becomes uneconomical to hold more stock in order to gain a little extra security of being able to satisfy demand.

Assume that the stock controller wants to hold enough stock to ensure that there is a 90 per cent probability that stock-outs will be avoided. An example may clarify this statement. Suppose that the monthly sales of a particular item for the past two and a half years have been as follows:

```
10  15  12   8  11   7   2  16  20  10  11  12
 6   5  13  10  11  15  20   9  11  15  10   5
14  10   6  20  13   8
```

Only three times in the past thirty months have the sales exceeded 16. If the lead time is one month, and the stock controller follows the rule that he makes an order when the stock drops to 16, then there will be a 10 per cent chance of an out-of-stock occurring during the lead time. This defines more precisely the previous statement that enough stock must be held to cover the maximum likely demand; the likelihood has been set at a numerical value, in this case 90 per cent probability.

Notice that in this example the most likely sales figure is 11, which is the average monthly sale. If an order is placed when the stock drops to 11, then there is an equal chance of demand exceeding the available stock or being less than the stock. Thus the stock controller can change the probability of a stock-out from 50 per cent to 10 per cent by setting the target stock level (often called the 'order point') five units higher, at 16 instead of 11. The most likely sales value is still 11, so that on average there will be 5 items in stock when the order arrives. This excess remaining stock at the time of delivery is known as the 'safety stock', and the larger the safety stock for a given item, the smaller the probability of a stock-out.

However, the objective we have been considering is not entirely satisfactory. The efficiency of the stock controller is better assessed by the service level he provides to the customers than by the number of stock-outs which occur. We are not so interested in the number of times he runs out of stock as in the total demand which is lost, or otherwise affected, by the stock-outs. There must be a measure of how serious a stock-out is likely to be, as well as the probability of its occurrence.

Suppose that the stock controller in the example habitually orders a quantity such that he will make three orders per year on average. In this case, if he always orders 44 items whenever he decides to make an order, then he will need to order every four months or so (the average monthly sale is 11). This means that he will have to risk an out-of-stock situation on three occasions per year. At any individual time when the stock drops to the critical level of 16, and an order is made, there is a 10 per cent probability of a stock-out. How serious will this stock-out be? In the past, when demand has been greater than 16, it has always been four units over 16. In the 10 per cent of cases where a stock-out occurs, the demand is likely to exceed the stock by four units. So the probable lost sales every time the stock controller has to make an order are 0·4. The risk of losing sales is taken three times per year. Therefore the annual lost sales under the strategy described are 1·2 on average. The average annual demand is about 130, so that the service level (sales divided by demand) is likely to be 128·8/130, or approximately 99 per cent.

Notice that the probability of a stock-out at any individual order time (90 per cent) is very different from the ultimate level of service given for the item in question (99 per cent). The level of service is a more complex concept than the probability of stock-out. It depends upon what is likely to happen on average over a large period of time, given a certain set of ordering rules.

In the above example it can be seen that, for a particular item with a given characteristic sales pattern, an order point of 16 units gives a probability of stock-out of 90 per cent each time an order is placed, but, coupled with an order-quantity rule that 44 units are ordered whenever an order is placed, the item would operate at a service level of about 99 per cent.

There are complex interactions between the order-point rule chosen, with its consequent safety stock level, the order quantity used, the sales pattern of the item and the service level that is likely to result. These interactions can be approached gradually through the use of examples. Before this is done, it is important to establish that the level of service as we have defined it is in fact the best criterion to use in evaluating the stock performance of an item. The assumption underlying the use of service level as a criterion of performance is that the amount of demand lost during stock-outs is important, as well as how often they occur. The inventory is therefore evaluated on the percentage of lost demand, or, more exactly, the percentage of demand not satisfied immediately from stock.

Service levels can be calculated in a number of different ways. The most common method of calculation is to divide sales by demand. It is sometimes convenient to calculate the lost sales and obtain the service from this, according to the following equation:

$$\text{service} = \text{sales}/(\text{sales} + \text{lost sales})$$

using the fact that demand equals (sales plus lost sales).

In the final analysis, the measure of inventory performance will be provided by the total service level maintained from the large groups of items comprising the total inventory. When the total inventory consists of many different items at different prices, several kinds of service level can be calculated. For example, the service level in units (unit sales divided by unit demand) will probably be different from the service level in value (£ sales divided by £ demand), according as the more expensive items are held at higher or lower individual service levels than the cheaper items. Both these measures of service are of interest under various circumstances, and a service level is generally most significant as a summary showing the total perfor-mance of a large number of items. In the close analysis of service level concepts in this chapter, we are using the service level figure to signify the probable future relations between sales and demand for a given item. As we are dealing with one single item at a constant price, the service level in units will be the same as the service level in value.

The following section considers the interactions between order points, order quantities and service levels in greater depth, using numerical examples. As a basis for these examples, some assumptions will be made about the characteristics of the items shown. It is assumed that the sales of the item in question vary around a constant level, and that the pattern of fluctuations around the basic level will be consistent. This is, of course, very rarely true in practice, but the example will provide valuable illustration. Further complications will have to be added to the theories expounded in order to deal with the real-life situation where demand patterns and levels are always changing.

Below is shown a demand history for one item. Sixty periods of history are provided, and it is assumed that any conclusions drawn from the analysis of this demand history will remain true for the performance of the item in the near future.

MONTHLY DEMAND HISTORY (ITEM A)

Year 1	4	7	5	2	9	8	3	6	5	6		8
Year 2	6	1	10	8	5	7	4	8	4	7	6	7
Year 3	2	8	6	5	6	4	5	5	11	6	3	5
Year 4	7	5	4	9	7	6	9	10	4	8	6	3
Year 5	5	7	3	7	5	6	9	2	3	7	4	6

As a first attempt at providing an ordering rule for item A, let us examine the probable consequences of the following strategy on the service level of the item: an order point of 7 and an order quantity of 12. That is to say, the stock controller will make an order immediately the stock drops to 7, and when this occurs he will order 12 units.

As the order quantity is 12, and the average monthly sales are 6, then *on average* an order will be placed every two months – six orders per year. Every time the order situation occurs there will be 7 items in stock. It is assumed that the lead time for this item is exactly one month (again not entirely a realistic situation).

There are 13 occasions in the demand history when the sales were more than 7. It can therefore be said that there are 13 chances out of 60 that, in a typical month, the sales will exceed 7. However, we are more interested in the amount of out-of-stock that will occur. On those 13 occasions, the extent of the out-of-stock situation in each case was as follows:

lost sales of 1 . . . . 6 times
lost sales of 2 . . . . 4 times
lost sales of 3 . . . . 2 times
lost sales of 4 . . . . 1 time.

Consequently, in any given month (and the lead time is one month) there is

1 chance in 60 of losing 4 sales
2 chances in 60 of losing 3 sales
4 chances in 60 of losing 2 sales

and 6 chances in 60 of losing 1 sale, giving a total probability of lost sales of

$$\left(\frac{1}{60} \times 4\right) + \left(\frac{2}{60} \times 3\right) + \left(\frac{4}{60} \times 2\right) + \left(\frac{6}{60} \times 1\right)$$

$$= 0 \cdot 067 + 0 \cdot 1 + 0 \cdot 133 + 0 \cdot 1 = 0 \cdot 4.$$

Thus, at any one order, the expected lost sales are 0·4. There are six orders per year, so that the average lost sales per year will be 2·4. The average yearly demand is 72, so that the level of service can be calculated as equal to (demand minus lost sales) divided by demand. This is equal to 69·6/72, or 96·7 per cent service.

What will be the effect of cutting the order quantity to 6? Firstly, the number of orders per year will become 12, so that an order is made every month on average. The number of sales lost in any individual order situation will remain as before, because the order point and the lead time are unchanged, but there will be more order situations. The probable lost sales per year now become 12 × 0·4 instead of 6 × 0·4 because of the larger number of orders placed. Therefore, if the order quantity is cut to 6, the service level will be (sales/demand) 67·2/72 or 93·3 per cent service. Fig. 1 shows the effect of different order quantities on the service level for this item, when the order point is kept at 7.

What happens now if the order point is varied rather than the order quantity? Using the previous order quantity of 12 units, implying 6 orders per year, what is the effect of reducing the order point to 6?

For item A there were 22 months in the demand history where demand was greater than 6, and the relative frequencies of different stock-out levels were as follows:

Demand	Number of occurrences	Lost sales	Probability	Probability × lost sales
7	9	1	9/60 = 0·15	0·15
8	6	2	6/60 = 0·10	0·20
9	4	3	4/60 = 0·07	0·20
10	2	4	2/60 = 0·03	0·13
11	1	5	1/60 = 0·017	0·08
			expected lost sales	0·75

This order situation occurs six times per year, so that yearly lost sales are 4·5. This gives a service level of 67·5/72 or 93·8 per cent, as opposed to 96·7 per cent for an order point of 7. Fig. 2 shows a graph of the effect of order point on service level for a fixed order quantity.

The method of calculation shown above is somewhat misleading

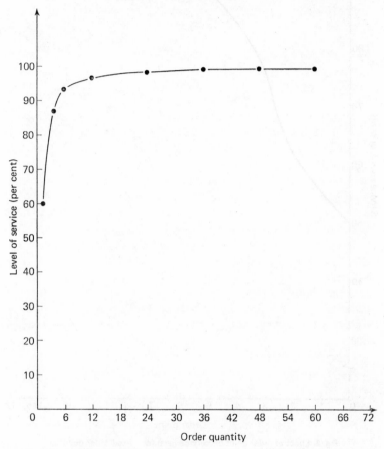

Fig. 1. Effect of order quantity on service level for a fixed order point

for very low order points, so that the graph in Fig. 2 shows a lower service level than the true value for these low order points. The reason for this becomes apparent if we examine the case where the order point is zero. In this case, a new order will be placed as soon as the stock runs out completely, and the true service level will be

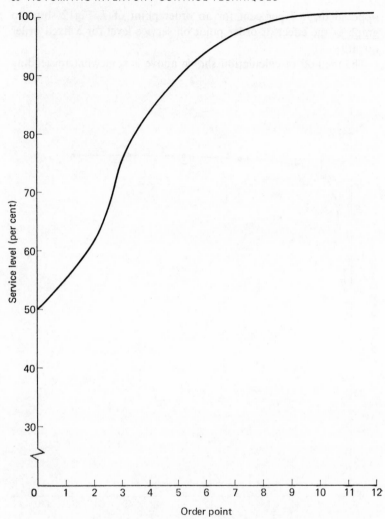

Fig. 2. Effect of order point on service level for a fixed order quantity

67 per cent. There is an implicit assumption in the method of calculation used above which breaks down for low service levels; this
is that if the order quantity is 12, then the number of orders per year
will be 6. In fact there will be only four orders per year when the
order point is zero and the order quantity is 12. Suppose that 12
units arrive in stock at month 1; these will sell out during months 1

and 2. A stock-out situation will obtain throughout month 3, and 12 more units will arrive in stock at the beginning of month 4. Another order will be made at the beginning of month 6, and the stock will again be zero during month 6; more merchandise will arrive at the beginning of month 7, and another order will be made at month 9. Likewise, another order will be made at month 12. Fig. 3 shows this situation in diagrammatic form.

The problem is that the low service level has reduced the sales so much that there are no longer about 6 orders per year from an order quantity of 12; the annual sales have been reduced to 48,

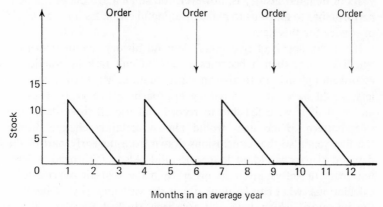

Fig. 3. Behaviour of ordering cycle with order point of zero

giving 4 orders per year. Nevertheless, the graph in Fig. 2 does apply correctly if full back-ordering is assumed, so that sales do not fall off in proportion to the service level. If back-orders are acceptable to the customers, then the normal two-month sales will be squeezed into the one month when stock is available, so that there will still be 6 orders per year, giving a service level of 50 per cent, as shown in Fig. 2. This problem is generally negligible, as few companies like to operate at a service level low enough to make this effect significant.

The method which has been used to calculate the service levels resulting from individual ordering strategies applied to item A has one important fallacy. The amount of demand history provided for the item is limited. If ten years of history were available for item A instead of five, it is quite likely that sales of zero or 12 might have occurred in one of the months. In the five years' history provided, the largest monthly demand is 11, and the smallest is 1. Sales of zero or 12 are quite possible from this item, but they have not occurred in the limited history available.

In particular, there is still a probability that sales of 12 or 13 may occur in the future performance of item A, although this probability is quite small. If sales of 12 or 13 were included in the calculations made above, the resultant service level figures would be significantly different, especially for high service levels. If the five years' history available is taken as being absolutely true, then it would be possible to provide 100 per cent service by using an order point of 11. Five years of demand history is, however, too small a sample of the item performance to allow us to make meaningful estimates for high levels of service for this item.

If we can speak of five years' demand history for an item as a 'small sample', then it becomes a very difficult task in practice to record enough history to give an exact solution. Most stock controllers would never retain anything approaching five years' history; and even if it were feasible to record and use all these data, the sales pattern of the item would almost certainly change during the five years, so that conclusions drawn from the early part of the demand history would no longer be valid. Also, if we need at least ten years of information in order to make realistic service level calculations, what can be done about the vast majority of items in the inventory which have not yet been stocked for the full ten years?

The method of calculation used so far, while useful for demonstration purposes, is very rarely of practical value as a stock-control method. Because of these objections to the simple approach to inventory control, more complex methods are used which are apparently less accurate and less satisfactory, but which can be applied to the practical situation where 'limited' historical information is available and demand patterns and levels are constantly changing. A discussion of these methods involves the use of simple probability distributions.

Before moving on to the more complex methods, let us formalize the method that was used above to calculate the effect of different order points and order quantities. A histogram of the number of months in which a particular sales value occurred will show the pattern drawn in Fig. 4. This is built up from the demand history as follows:

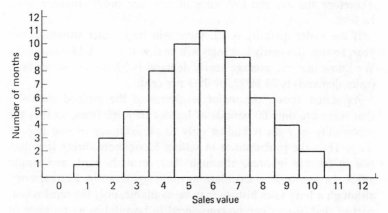

Demand value	Number of occurrences
0	0
1	1
2	3
3	5
4	8
5	10
6	11
7	9
8	6
9	4
10	2
11	1
12	0
Total	60

Fig. 4. Histogram of demand

The critical figure in calculating service level is the lost demand which is likely to occur in any ordering situation. It is therefore convenient to turn the above table of occurrences into a table of probabilities for each of the sales values. This is done by dividing each of the entries for the number of occurrences by the total number of observations; that is, we divide each entry by 60 to arrive at the probability of occurrence of each of the sales values (see table overleaf).

It can then be said that if the order point is set at 8, there is a probability of 0·07 of losing 1 sale, a probability of 0·03 of losing 2 sales and a probability of 0·02 of losing 3 sales. In other words, in 100 different order situations, there would be 7 cases where 1 sale was lost, 3 cases where 2 sales were lost, and 2 cases where 3 sales

Sales value	Probability
0	0·00
1	0·02
2	0·05
3	0·08
4	0·13
5	0·17
6	0·18
7	0·15
8	0·10
9	0·07
10	0·03
11	0·02
12	0·00

were lost. Total lost sales in 100 situations would be $7 + 6 + 6 = 19$. Therefore the average lost sales in any one order situation must be 0·19.

If the order quantity is 12, there will be 6 order situations per year, so that the yearly lost sales will be $6 \times 0·19 = 1·14$ on average. We know that the average yearly demand is 72, so the service level (sales/demand) is 70·86/72, or 98·3 per cent.

As stated above, the major weakness of the method shown is that there are only 60 periods of history to work from, so that the probability of sales is known only to an accuracy of one part in sixty. Thus the probabilities of selling 12 or more, being less than one in 60, are ignored, although they certainly exist, and would affect the service level calculations quite significantly. Furthermore, although a long sales history may be available, only the most recent part of that history can be considered to be valid as an estimate of what will happen in the future, because the demand pattern is likely to have changed during the life of the item. It would of course be possible to create a larger amount of history artificially by recording sales at weekly instead of monthly intervals, thus multiplying the amount of data by four. Although this is superficially attractive, the difficulty is that the lead time has been defined as one month, so that we need to know the likely sales *during a month*; it is of marginal value to have a finer breakdown of sales for this purpose.

There is very little hope of accumulating enough sales values to provide even an approximately correct estimate of the pattern of probabilities of sales of any one item. Another approach has to be taken. In the absence of sufficient information to make a complete table of the probable sales of an item, the probability pattern or 'distribution' is assumed to conform to some standard probability distribution. The advantage of this is that the low probability values at the tail end of the pattern can be filled in from the theoretical shape of the distribution, without having to wait for one of the unlikely sales actually to occur before taking its probability into account. The disadvantage is that the 'true' shape of the sales probability distribution may not conform to the theoretical model which is being used. In practice it is found that sales patterns do conform closely enough to one of a small number of different standard distributions to make any errors involved marginal; the advantages of using a theoretical distribution therefore far outweigh the disadvantages.

It is unusual to use a distribution of probable *sales* for stock-control purposes. The effects of changes in demand level, uptrends and downtrends, and seasonal cycles in demand would be to scatter sales across the probability distribution. For example, the sales of an item which had an average monthly demand of 10 units per month during 1965 and 20 units per month during 1966 would give the shape shown in Fig. 5. Alternatively, an item with a straight uptrend and no random fluctuations at all – sales of 21, 22, 23, 24, etc., in successive months, for example – would show a very spread distribution pattern.

For these reasons, it is usual to assume that some *forecast* can be made of what the demand level is likely to be, which must take into account changes in level, trends and seasonal patterns, and to use a probability distribution of sales around the forecast.

If it is known that a particular item sells on average 10 units in January, 20 units in February and so on, according to the following seasonal cycle:

Month	Seasonal average	Actual sales 1966	Fluctuation around forecast
1	10	9	−1
2	20	20	0
3	30	31	+1
4	25	26	+1
5	20	18	−2
6	10	12	+2
7	5	4	−1
8	5	3	−2
9	10	10	0
10	20	20	0
11	40	41	+1
12	15	14	−1

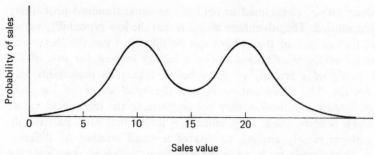

Fig. 5. Distribution of sales with yearly average of 10, then 20, units

then the distribution around the seasonal forecast is the most useful to calculate, and would show the following pattern:

```
            X     X     X
      X     X     X     X
      X     X     X     X     X

     −2    −1  Forecast  +1    +2
```

This is a much more compact and easily used curve than the actual distribution of sales.

This introduces a further complexity into mathematical stock-control systems: some forecast has to be made of what the demand level is likely to be. It will be assumed for the moment that there is some method of producing a 'reliable' forecast, which will enable us to predict some of the fluctuations in demand – seasonal cycles, uptrends, changes in level, etc. There will be other fluctuations which are either random or not predictable by mathematical techniques. These fluctuations make up the probability distribution of variations from forecast. It is common practice to call the difference between actual sales and forecast the 'forecast error', although a mathematician would probably claim that any error introduced was the fault of the demand rather than the forecast. Techniques of forecasting will be discussed in Chapter 4.

What are the characteristics of the theoretical forecast error distribution that will be used for stock-control purposes? If the forecasting method is reasonably good it should strike fairly close to the centre of the probability distribution. The point of highest probability on the distribution should correspond with a forecast error of zero. If the forecast errors are consistently to one side of the zero point, then the forecasting method is biased and not performing well. This is illustrated in Fig. 6. The theoretical probability distribution used should have its highest point at the centre, where the forecast error is zero.

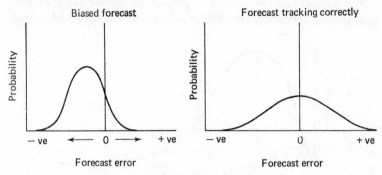

Fig. 6. Distribution of forecast error

The distribution most often used to represent the probability distribution of forecast errors for stock-control purposes is the 'normal' distribution, whose characteristic bell-shaped curve is shown in Fig. 7. This distribution is completely symmetrical around the centre point, so that sales are assumed to be equally likely to be above or below forecast, and equally likely to be, say, 10 above fore-

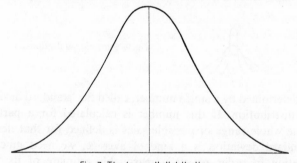

Fig. 7. The 'normal' distribution

cast as 10 below forecast. This seems to work well except when the average sales are very low. The problem is that it is impossible to sell less than zero. If the average sales are, say, 2 per month, probabilities of a forecast error of more than −2 do not exist, but it is perfectly possible to sell 5, giving a forecast error of +3. In this case, other statistical distributions such as Poisson distributions are used, with the general shape shown in Fig. 8. The normal distribution is more commonly used, and will serve as an illustration of how statistical distributions are used in stock control.

The normal distribution has to provide an infinite range of possible shapes, depending on whether sales are widely scattered around

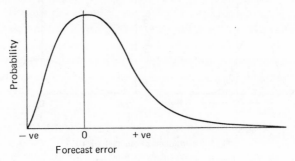

Fig. 8. Poisson distribution

the forecast or closely grouped around it. Fig. 9 shows some normal distributions. Notice that they all have the standard bell shape, but they vary according as the demand is more or less widely spread around the forecast.

The shape which a normal distribution will take in any individual

Fig. 9. Some normal distributions

case is determined by a single number, called the 'standard deviation' of the distribution. If this number is calculated for a particular item, the whole range of possible sales is defined for that item. As the standard deviation is a kind of average, we need much less information in order to get a reasonable estimate of its value; this method is therefore usable in the normal stock-control situation.

The standard deviation of the forecast error distribution of an item can be calculated as follows: make a list of the forecast errors for each time-period in the demand history; square each of the individual forecast errors; find the average value of these squared forecast errors; take the square root of this average. This number is the standard deviation. The standard deviation will be small if the forecasts have been reasonably accurate, and the sales are grouped closely around the forecast; it will be large if the sales are widely scattered. A small standard deviation will give a tall, narrow probability distribution; a large one will give a low, wide distribution.

It is often too unwieldy and time-consuming to calculate the standard deviation of forecast errors. Fortunately, the standard deviation can be estimated quite accurately from another figure, which is very easy to calculate. This is the 'mean absolute deviation' (commonly abbreviated to MAD). The MAD is nothing more than the average error which has occurred, ignoring the sign of the error. Thus, if an item has performed as follows:

Forecast	Sales	Forecast error	Absolute error
10	12	+2	2
11	8	−3	3
16	16	0	0
15	16	+1	1
10	9	−1	1
11	11	0	0
12	10	−2	2
15	16	+1	1
15	15	0	0
14	13	−1	1
		Total	11

then the mean absolute deviation (the average absolute error) is 1·1. (Note that the word 'absolute', in a mathematical context, means 'ignoring the sign'.) It has been found that the standard deviation of a normal distribution is about 1·25 MAD. For the demand history above, the standard deviation of forecast errors could be approximated as 1·38. This figure defines the forecast error distribution precisely, although several approximations have been used in arriving at the result, so that it will only be accurate within certain limits. This technique works quite accurately enough for most stock-control purposes, despite the theoretical objections, which are:

No real distribution of sales is likely to correspond exactly to a normal distribution.

The MAD has been calculated on the basis of ten historical values, whereas the 'true' average error may be slightly different from this figure.

An approximate rule has been used for deciding the standard

A.I.C.T.—4

deviation from the MAD. (But the stated value of 1·25 is an approximate figure which covers the majority of cases reasonably well.)

If this technique can give a usable estimate of the probability distribution of forecast errors, how can this be used to estimate service levels and order points? One obvious approach would be to generate the different probabilities of sales from the forecast and the standard deviation, and to operate as before, calculating first the annual probable lost sales, and then the order points and service levels from this and from the annual demand.

There is a large amount of calculation involved in generating all the separate probability values for a wide range of possible sales. Fortunately the normal distribution has been studied extensively by statisticians, and they have developed short cuts which do not involve the generation of all the separate probabilities.

The first useful statement that can be made about the normal distribution is that 68 per cent of the sales values will be within one standard deviation of the centre point (i.e. the forecast), 95 per cent of the sales will be within two standard deviations of the forecast, and 99 per cent within three standard deviations. Intermediate values can of course be calculated also: the percentage of cases covered by taking, for example, 1½ standard deviations from the centre point can be found from statistical tables. It will be somewhere between 68 per cent and 95 per cent, but nearer 95 per cent.

These facts can at least define the probability of a stock-out occurring. For example, the following sales history will be used to show some actual figures:

FORECAST DEMAND: 100 PER MONTH

Month	1	2	3	4	5	6	7	8	9	10
Demand	100	90	80	110	90	120	130	70	100	100
Forecast error	0	−10	−20	+10	−10	+20	+30	−30	0	0

The mean absolute deviation is 13, so that the standard deviation is approximately 16·3. If the lead time is one month, and an order point of 116 is used, then we can be sure that just under 68 per cent of the sales will be between 84 and 116 per month (forecast plus or minus one standard deviation), so that no stock-outs occur. In the remaining 32 per cent of cases, half of these sales will be below 84, and half above 116. Therefore there will be an out-of-stock situation in 16 per cent of the order situations. In the sample sales history, sales of more than 116 occurred twice out of ten sales, which corresponds closely to our theoretical estimate. Likewise, if an order point of 133 is used – two standard deviations from the forecast – there will be stock-outs in $\frac{1}{2}(100 - 95) = 2\frac{1}{2}$ per cent of cases. The number of out-of-stock situations is less important than the total demand lost by stock-outs, as has been shown previously, so that calculations should be based on service levels rather than percentage stock-outs.

We therefore need to compute the total probable lost sales represented by setting an order point a certain number of standard deviations above the forecast. This is more complex, and involves multiplying the probability of each individual sale by the number of lost sales it represents. The most common method of deciding what should be the order point to provide a given service level is as follows. Firstly a figure called the service function is calculated:

$$\text{service function} = \frac{\text{order quantity (100 per cent} - \text{desired service)}}{\text{standard deviation}}.$$

Then a standard statistical table is used to find the number of standard deviations above the forecast required in the order point. Some entries from this standard table are shown below. K is the number of standard deviations to be included in the order point.

K	Service function
0·0	0·4
0·5	0·2
1·0	0·08
1·5	0·03
2·0	0·008
2·5	0·002
3·0	0·0005
3·5	0·00007

In order to demonstrate the use of this table, we shall return to the sales history of item A, from which results of different order points and order quantities were calculated, using the simple probability method. In order to employ the new technique, the standard deviation must be calculated, and a forecast of demand made from the item. Here is the item demand history repeated:

Year 1	4	7	5	2	9	8	3	6	5	6	4	8
Year 2	6	1	10	8	5	7	4	8	4	7	6	7
Year 3	2	8	6	5	6	4	5	5	11	6	3	5
Year 4	7	5	4	9	7	6	9	10	4	8	6	3
Year 5	5	7	3	7	5	6	9	2	3	7	4	6

The average monthly demand for this item is 6 units. The mean absolute deviation, or average forecast error (ignoring sign), is 1·7, therefore the standard deviation is about 1·25 × 1·7, or approximately 2·0. The first example using probability techniques arrived at a service level of 96·7 per cent from an order quantity of 12 and an order point of 7. Let us calculate from our improved method, which takes into account the full probability distribution of sales, what order point *should* produce a service level of 96·7 per cent under those conditions.

The first figure to be calculated is the service function:

$$\frac{\text{order quantity} = 12}{\text{standard deviation} = 2} \quad (100 \text{ per cent} - \text{service level}$$

$$= 96·7 \text{ per cent})$$
$$= 6 × 3·3 \text{ per cent} = 0·198.$$

From the service function table it can be seen that 0·5 standard deviations are required, so that the order point is the forecast (6) plus 0·5 times the standard deviation (2). Thus our theoretical order point corresponds exactly with the order point previously calculated (7).

As the service level becomes higher, we approach closer to the tail of the probability distribution, and the values of unlikely sales which simply have not occurred in the 'limited' history sample of five years' demand become more and more significant. The graph of service levels against order points in Fig. 2 gives a very high service level for an order point of 9 – well above 99·5 per cent. Using the new theoretical approach, we can work out the real consequences of this order point.

With an order point of 9, there are $1\frac{1}{2}$ standard deviations above the forecast, so that K is 1·5 in the service function table. This implies a service function value of 0·03. The resultant service level can then be calculated from the equation:

$$0·03 = \frac{12 \,(100 \text{ per cent} - \text{service level})}{2}$$

so that service = 100 per cent − 0·03/6 = 99·5 per cent.

Certainly an order point of 11 will not give 100 per cent service, as would be implied by the fact that no sale over 11 occurred in the five years' history. This service level can be calculated by the same method:

order point = forecast + K times standard deviation

$$11 = 6 + 2K$$

so that $K = 2.5$.

The corresponding service function value is 0·002.

So $0.002 = 6$ (100 per cent − service)

and service $= 100$ per cent − 0·2 per cent/6 = 99·97 per cent

which is very different from 100 per cent service.

It is interesting to note that the sample item A has a forecast error distribution which does not correspond exactly with the normal distribution. From the histogram in Fig. 4 it can be seen that the sales are not symmetrically distributed around the average. Nevertheless, the assumption of a normal distribution has given results which are very close to those calculated from the actual sales.

This demonstrates a short-cut method of calculating order points and service. The main question left unanswered is, what is the meaning of the service function table? In simple terms, the service function is the expected lost sales per order, adjusted for expected frequency of ordering, and divided by the standard deviation. The reason for this is that if any normal distribution is plotted on a scale marked out in standard deviations, it always comes down to exactly the same shape and size of curve. One single table of lost sales versus K factor can therefore be used for all cases, providing the distribution is marked out in terms of the standard deviation (divided by the standard deviation). Once the K factor has been found, it is multiplied by the standard deviation to produce a result applicable to the particular distribution in question. It is not necessary to follow all the details of the service function table. What is important is to notice the effects on the order point of the three major factors − service level, order quantity and standard deviation.

If the service level is raised, then the term (100 per cent − service level) will decrease. Therefore the service function will decrease. The service function is some measure of probable lost sales. If probable lost sales are small, then a large K factor is required to produce more stock − in other words, as the service function increases, K decreases, and vice versa. Thus a smaller service function produces a larger K. Now the order point is equal to the forecast plus K standard deviations. If K increases, the stock increases. In summary, a higher service level causes higher stocks, as one would expect.

If the order quantity increases, the service function increases. A large allowable lost sales means a small K factor. Therefore the order point decreases if the order quantity increases. This is reasonable because there will be fewer order situations per year if the order quantity is large, so that we can afford to hold smaller safety stocks and allow a larger probability of lost sales on the few occasions where an order situation does arise.

If the standard deviation of forecast errors increases, the service function will decrease, so that the K factor will increase. Thus the standard deviation is extremely significant in determining the amount of safety stock that must be held. If the standard deviation increases, it will cause stock to increase, because the order point is made up of the forecast plus K standard deviations. However, the increase in standard deviation will *also* cause an increased K factor. This means that the accuracy of the forecasting method used is the most significant factor affecting the order point. If the forecast is accurate, the spread of forecast errors will be small, resulting in small stocks. If the forecast is inaccurate, giving a wide spread of forecast errors, the effect on stocks will be more than proportional to the increased inaccuracy. This is why so much emphasis is placed on methods of demand forecasting in stock-control theory.

To summarize, then:

Order point = forecast + K standard deviations.

K is found from a table of K in relation to service function, such that a high service function gives a low K, and a low service function a high K.

$$\text{Service function} = \frac{\text{order quantity } (1 - \text{service level})}{\text{standard deviation of forecast errors}}.$$

Increased service level means increased order points.
Increased order quantities mean decreased order points.
Increased standard deviations mean greatly increased order points.

It is worth noting that the part of the order point made up by K standard deviations is frequently called the 'safety stock'. This is the average amount of stock remaining when the order arrives, and thus directly affects the average stock level. Normally safety stocks make up a large proportion of the total value of an inventory, usually of the order of 40 per cent.

In this chapter we have discussed a mathematical technique for setting stock levels. What happens in practice with most manual stock-control situations, where the stock controller does not have time to perform complex calculations? It is very common for a stock-control rule of the following kind to be applied: 'When the stock drops to 5 weeks' supply, then reorder.' This is a method which relies on the stock controller's forecast of sales alone, and takes no account of the possible variability in demand. It is effectively an order-point rule which, if the lead time is four weeks, has the following form:

order point = forecast (lead time) + forecast (1 week).

There is a wide range of variabilities in the sales of different items. An item that is easy to forecast, with small deviations between sales and forecast, will operate at a high service level under this kind of ordering rule. An item with highly variable sales will operate at a low service level. Thus the effect of the manual ordering rule is to give a wide range of service levels over different items in the inventory, from which some average overall service level will result. It can be shown that this is a very inefficient method of providing service to customers, and is very wasteful of stock. A more precise inventory control system can save money from the inventory in several different ways. However, two major possible savings can be seen immediately. Firstly, a more accurate forecasting system can drastically reduce the safety stock required to provide a given level of service; secondly, stock can be saved by using it more efficiently to provide a *consistent* service level for every item. In order to demonstrate this second more clearly, consider an inventory composed entirely of two items, A and B. We shall assume that these items are very similar in nature, that they have the same annual sales, price, lead time and order quantity, but that item A's demand pattern is slightly more variable than that of item B. Suppose that £1,000 of stock of item A is held, giving an effective service level of

90 per cent, and there is £1,000 of stock of item B, giving a service level of 98 per cent. These figures are tabulated below:

	Average stock value	Service level (per cent)
Item A	£1,000	90
Item B	£1,000	98
Total stock	£2,000	average service 94

These figures could well be the result of an 'order when stock is down to five weeks' supply' policy applied to both items.

Suppose now that we decide to invest more stock in item A. In order to raise item A's service level to 94 per cent, we might have to increase the stock by £200. Thus item A would have a stock of £1,200 and a service level of 94 per cent. Because there are always diminishing returns from increased safety stock, an extra unit of safety stock brings in less and less extra service as the service level increases, so that it costs much more stock to move from 94 per cent to 98 per cent than it does to move from 90 per cent to 94 per cent. Thus the savings from reducing item B's service level to 94 per cent would be much more than £200; they might well be of the order of £400. This gives a new stock investment situation:

	Average stock value	Service level (per cent)
Item A	£1,200	94
Item B	£600	94

The average service level for the whole inventory is still 94 per cent, and we are giving the same customer satisfaction and capturing the same proportion of the demand. However, the total stock value is now £1,800 instead of £2,000. A considerable saving has been achieved by balancing the item service levels correctly.

It is not necessarily true that the most profitable policy is to hold all items at the same level of service. It is true in our example where the items have been defined as being very similar in nature. If the sales rates or profit margins vary significantly among the items in the inventory, it may be more profitable to hold them at different levels of service. Once the most profitable service level for a particular item has been discovered, it can be maintained at this level by techniques such as the one described in this chapter, so as to produce large overall stock savings or service level increases or both. The decision as to the ideal service level balance for items of widely varying characteristics will be discussed at a later stage when more of the significant factors in inventory efficiency have been dealt with.

The next major factor to be considered in an automatic inventory control system is the forecasting method used. Before this subject is introduced, the effect of several other factors on order points and safety stocks will be analysed.

Firstly, it has been assumed in all the examples so far that we were provided with monthly demand information about an item, and that the lead time was one month. This makes it very simple to calculate safety stocks and variability, because we require to know only the forecast demand and the probable variability in demand during the lead time, and these factors can be obtained directly from the demand history. Suppose that the lead time is $2\frac{1}{2}$ months. It is relatively easy to expand the forecast over this interval: it is only necessary to add together the forecast for next month and the month after, and then add half the forecast for the third month. On the other hand it is difficult to know the variability over the $2\frac{1}{2}$-month lead time; the MAD over the new period will not be $2\frac{1}{2}$ times greater than the one-month MAD. It will in fact be somewhat greater than the MAD for a period of one month (but not $2\frac{1}{2}$ times greater), as the forecasts will be somewhat less accurate over the longer period. In order to discover what is the loss of accuracy with increased time, it is normal to classify items into groups and study what occurs in practice with a particular forecasting method. If this is not possible, a rule of thumb that seems to be reasonably accurate for the vast majority of cases is to assume that the forecast inaccuracy increases according to the square root of the time period. That is, if the forecasts are made monthly, and the lead time is four months, then the MAD over the lead time will be approximately twice the monthly MAD; if the lead time were nine months, the variability would be three times greater than the monthly figure, and so on.

The most costly effect of a long lead time can often be the chance of the demand for a product falling off drastically between the placing of an order and the receipt of the merchandise, which would result in an over-stock situation which would take a long time to rectify itself. There is always a finite possibility for any item that such a rapid falling-off in demand may occur.

This leads to the rather surprising conclusion that the length of the lead time does not directly affect the average inventory level. The effect of changing one's supplier from one with a two-month lead time to one with a four-month lead time should not require very much more stock. Overall, the forecast errors will be about 1·4 times as big, which might increase the safety stock by a factor of 1·6. If 40 per cent of the inventory is safety stock, then the total effect on inventory will be a 24 per cent increase. It can be far more costly to the stock controller if the lead time is erratic, because he must plan for the maximum likely lead time, and the deliveries will often arrive before time, while there is still a fair amount of stock remaining. This may increase the average stock holding considerably. The actual effect of length and variability of lead time will depend on the particular characteristics of the items concerned, but it may prove advantageous to obtain a consistent but long lead time rather than an erratic but short one. In summary, if the lead time is different from the forecast interval, the forecast errors will have to be expanded or contracted to fit the lead time. In the absence of a study in the particular situation it is often sufficiently accurate to assume that the forecast error varies according to the square root of the time-period.

Another factor which has been avoided so far in the examples given is the effect of the review interval. Up to now it has been assumed that the stock controller will know immediately when the order point is passed. This is not necessarily true in practice. Depending on the number of items to be controlled, their speed of movement, and the amount of time the stock controller has available, he will not be aware of the actual stock position of all the items at any one time. It is very common to take one section of the inventory each day and decide on orders for those items selected, then take another section the next day, and so on. If one-fifth of the items are analysed each day, then each item will be reviewed on average once a week. If only one-twentieth of the items can be handled in one day, the review time will be one month. This means that the stock controller has not only to allow for sales which will occur during the lead time, but must also allow for sales which will occur during the review time, before he has a chance to review the item again.

If, for example, an item sells at the steady rate of 10 per month, with insignificant variability, the lead time is one month and the review time is one month, and the stock controller allows only for the lead time, he will set an order point of 10. Suppose that the stock controller comes to review the item, and there are 11 in stock; if he believes his order point of 10, he will not order. One month later he will review the item again, and there will be only 1 unit in stock. It is then too late to avoid lost sales. Therefore allowance must be made for both the lead time and the review time in setting the order point.

The new order-point equation, taking these factors into account, becomes:

order point = forecast sales during lead time plus review time, plus K times the standard deviation of forecast errors likely to occur over the lead time plus review time

or, in shorter form:

$$OP = F(LT + RT) + K\sigma(LT + RT)$$

where σ (sigma) stands for standard deviation.

Chapter 4
Automatic Forecasting Systems

Many of the developments in forecasting systems have come from the area of stock control, where it has been very important to have some estimate of future item sales, so that enough stock is held to cover the expected demand. In stock control, how much stock do we need to have available at all times? Obviously enough to last until a new supply arrives. If it is assumed that there is no merchandise on order, that is, still to be delivered, we shall always need enough stock to last for one 'lead time', that is, to cover the period between making an order and receiving the delivery. In order to find out what this desired stock level is, it is necessary to make some estimate of future demand. Suppose, for example, that the lead time for a given article is two months. Then we need to have in stock at least the forecast sales for two months ahead. Our forecast may be more or less accurate, and we have to make allowance for this fact. Take an example where the past sales of an article, month by month, have been:

January	9	December	7
February	10	January	8
March	12	February	11
April	13	March	10
May	11	April	15
June	15	May	9
July	11	June	16
August	10	July	10
September	8	August	7
October	9	September	4
November	5		

This sales pattern is plotted in Fig. 10.
It can be seen that the average monthly sales have been 10, but

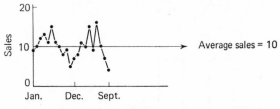

Fig. 10. Representative sales pattern

that the accuracy of this estimate in the past has been an error rate as follows:

January	1	December	3
February	0	January	2
March	2	February	1
April	3	March	0
May	1	April	5
June	5	May	1
July	1	June	6
August	0	July	0
September	2	August	3
October	1	September	6
November	5		

There is an average error of 48/21, i.e. 2·3 per month, so that the forecast for this item might be expressed as $10 \pm 2·3$.

Consequently we need a certain amount of extra 'buffer' stock in order to cover the probable forecast error. How much stock is required for this buffer which corresponds to the safety stock which has been discussed in previous chapters? It depends upon the average forecast error. Most stock-control requirements entail a measure of probability of being out of stock, that is, of exceeding a certain sales rate. If we draw a histogram of the sales in the example, we should expect to find the shape illustrated in Fig. 11. Notice that sales figures near the average occur most frequently, and larger errors are less frequent. It is usually assumed that the sales will be symmetrically distributed around the forecast, according to a 'normal' distribution, which has the shape drawn in Fig. 12. The average absolute error of the forecast, its 'mean absolute deviation' (MAD), provides a measure of the shape of this distribution. If the

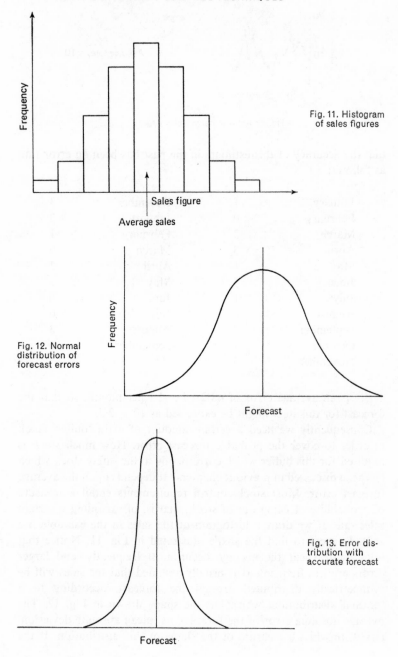

Fig. 11. Histogram of sales figures

Fig. 12. Normal distribution of forecast errors

Fig. 13. Error distribution with accurate forecast

MAD is small, then the sales will be closely grouped around the forecast, as in Fig. 13. With a large MAD the distribution will be widely spread, as in Fig. 14. In order to have a high probability of being in stock, it is necessary to hold several times MAD as safety stock.

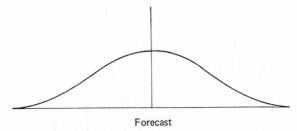

Forecast

Fig. 14. Error distribution with high variability

In order to be in stock, we need to have at least the forecast for the next two months – say 20 items – in stock, plus, say, 3 MADs for safety. 3 × 2·4 is approximately 7, so that total stock requirement is 27.

Supposing that the sales could be forecast as having a definite seasonal pattern, the forecasts would be more accurate. If we could express the shape of the series of historical sales figures as a combination of mathematical curves, we could make this fit much closer to the actual data. If seasonality did exist, we should be able to reduce the MAD. The sales history in the example has been chosen to show a sinusoidal pattern of frequency 1 per year, and an amplitude of about 5 (see p. 83).

In Fig. 15, the actual data are plotted against the function $a_1 + a_2 \sin(2\pi t/p)$, where the period p is 12 per annum, a_2 is the estimated amplitude of 5, and a_1 is the average sale (10).

$\sin 0° =$	0·0	$5 \sin(\pi t/6) =$	0·0
$\sin 30° =$	0·5	$=$	2·5
$\sin 60° =$	0·866	$=$	4·3
$\sin 90° =$	1·0	$=$	5·0
$\sin 120° =$	0·866	$=$	4·3
$\sin 150° =$	0·5	$=$	2·5
$\sin 180° =$	0·0	$=$	0·0
$\sin 210° =$	$-0·5$	$=$	$-2·5$
$\sin 240° =$	$-0·866$	$=$	$-4·3$
$\sin 270° =$	$-1·0$	$=$	$-5·0$

and so on.

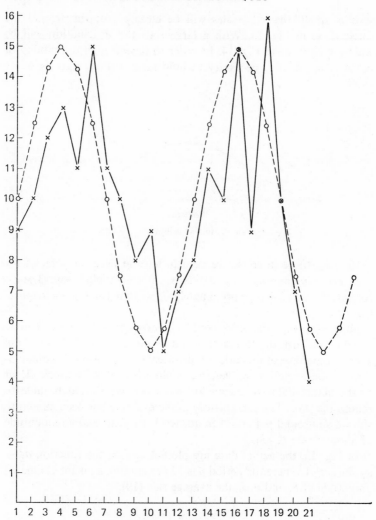

Fig. 15. Sine curve plotted against actual data

The errors are much smaller if we use the sine curve as our forecast. They are then 1, 2·5, 2·3, 2, 3·3, 2·5, 1, 2·5, 2·3, 4, 0·7, 0·5, 2, 1·5, 4·3, 0, 5·3, 3·5, 0, 0·3, 0·5 for each month respectively. The new MAD is 42/21, or 2·0. The new forecast for two months ahead is plotted in Fig. 15; it is 5 for October and 5·7 for November, giving a total of 10·7. To this must be added safety stock: $10·7 + (3 \times 2·0) \doteqdot$

SALES HISTORY 4: EXPONENTIAL SMOOTHING ($\alpha = 0.2$)

Period	Sales	Forecast	Error	MAD	CUSUM	SE
1	11	10·0	1·0	2·0	1·0	0·1
2	8	10·2	−2·2	1·9	−1·2	−0·1
3	15	9·8	5·2	1·9	4·0	0·4
4	10	10·8	−0·8	2·3	3·2	0·3
5	12	10·6	1·4	2·1	4·6	0·4
6	16	10·9	5·1	2·0	9·7	0·9
7	12	11·9	0·1	2·3	9·7	0·8
8	15	11·9	3·1	2·1	12·8	1·0
9	16	12·6	3·4	2·2	3·4	1·3
10	20	13·2	6·8	2·3	10·2	1·8
11	14	14·6	−0·6	2·8	9·6	1·6
12	17	14·5	2·5	2·6	12·1	1·7
13	20	15·0	5·0	2·6	17·1	2·0
14	16	16·0	0·0	2·8	0·0	1·8
15	22	16·0	6·0	2·5	6·0	2·2
16	25	17·2	7·8	2·9	13·8	2·8
17	21	18·8	2·2	3·4	16·1	2·7
18	18	19·2	−1·2	3·3	14·9	2·3
19	19	19·0	0·0	3·0	14·9	2·1
20	17	19·0	−2·0	2·7	12·9	1·7
21	20	18·6	1·4	2·7	14·4	1·7
22	21	18·9	2·1	2·5	16·5	1·7
23	21	19·3	1·7	2·5	1·7	1·7
24	21	19·6	1·4	2·4	3·1	1·7
25	15	19·9	−4·9	2·3	−1·8	1·0
26	20	18·9	1·1	2·6	−0·7	1·0
27	19	19·1	−0·1	2·4	−0·9	0·9
28	19	19·1	−0·1	2·2	−1·0	0·8
29	19	19·1	−0·1	2·0	−1·1	0·7
30	17	19·1	−2·1	1·8	−3·2	0·4
31	15	18·7	−3·7	1·8	−6·8	0·0
32	18	17·9	0·1	2·0	−6·7	0·0
33	12	17·9	−5·9	1·8	−12·7	−0·6
34	10	16·8	−6·8	2·2	−6·8	−1·2
35	11	15·4	−4·4	2·7	−11·2	−1·5
36	11	14·5	−3·5	2·9	−14·7	−1·7

These data are plotted in Fig. 17.

In this example, the CUSUM is reset to zero when the limit is reached. Four tracking signals were produced, and the drop in sales was detected at the end of the sales history; another tracking signal will probably occur in period 37. On the other hand, the smoothed-error tracking signal operated continuously until the forecast caught up with the sales and then switched itself off. The drop in sales is detected very quickly by the smoothed-error signal.

It was said previously that when the sales level changes, a high α factor should be used, and when sales are stable a low factor is required. We now have a method of detecting changes in level, so that the α factor can be adjusted continuously to correspond with the likelihood of a change in level. α must always be between 0 and 1, and the new tracking signal must also vary between 0 and 1. Tracking signal = SE/MAD, remembering that the smoothed error must always be less than the MAD. Trigg therefore suggests that the tracking signal be used as the α factor, so that the α automatically adjusts itself to the change in level.

This procedure should be much more effective than traditional methods of finding the 'best' α on average over the history, using time-consuming trial and error techniques. It is easy to calculate and produces a high α when fast response is needed, and a low α when stability is required, instead of relying on a fixed α for a given item.

The following table shows this technique in action on data which show a change in level, compared with a technique which has chosen the 'best' α factor and uses it throughout.

SALES HISTORY 5: TRIGG'S METHOD

Period	Sales	Forecast	Error	MAD	SE	α
1	12	10·0	2·0	2·0	0·2	0·10
2	9	10·2	−1·2	2·0	0·1	0·10
3	10	10·2	−0·2	1·9	0·0	0·03
4	8	10·2	−2·2	1·7	−0·2	0·02
5	9	9·9	−0·9	1·8	−0·3	0·10
6	15	9·8	5·2	1·7	0·3	0·15
7	11	10·5	0·5	2·1	0·3	0·14
8	10	10·6	−0·6	1·9	0·2	0·16
9	12	10·5	1·5	1·8	0·3	0·12
10	12	10·8	1·2	1·7	0·4	0·20
11	7	11·1	−4·1	1·7	−0·0	0·25
12	10	11·1	−1·1	1·9	−0·1	0·02
13	13	11·0	2·0	1·8	0·1	0·07
14	11	11·1	−0·1	1·9	0·1	0·04
15	8	11·1	−3·1	1·7	−0·2	0·04
16	13	10·7	2·3	1·8	0·0	0·14
17	10	10·7	−0·7	1·9	−0·1	0·01
18	14	10·6	3·4	1·7	0·3	0·03
19	20	11·2	8·8	1·9	1·1	0·15
20	24	15·0	9·0	2·6	1·9	0·44
21	16	20·4	−4·4	3·2	1·3	0·59
22	17	18·7	−1·7	3·4	1·0	0·39
23	20	18·1	1·9	3·2	1·1	0·31
24	19	18·8	0·2	3·1	1·0	0·36
25	22	18·9	3·1	2·8	1·2	0·36
26	20	20·2	−0·2	2·8	1·1	0·43
27	21	20·1	0·9	2·5	1·0	0·42
28	17	20·5	−3·5	2·4	0·6	0·44
29	18	19·7	−1·7	2·5	0·4	0·24
30	20	19·4	0·6	2·4	0·4	0·15
31	25	19·5	5·5	2·2	0·9	0·17
32	15	21·4	−6·4	2·5	0·2	0·35
33	20	21·1	−1·1	2·9	0·0	0·05
34	21	21·1	−0·1	2·8	0·0	0·01
35	22	21·1	0·9	2·5	0·1	0·01
36	21	21·1	−0·1	2·3	0·1	0·05

SALES HISTORY 5: EXPONENTIAL SMOOTHING ($\alpha = 0.25$)

Period	Sales	Forecast	Error	MAD	SE	Tracking signal
1	12	10·0	2·0	2·0	0·2	0·10
2	9	10·5	−1·5	2·0	0·0	0·01
3	10	10·1	−0·1	1·9	0·0	0·01
4	8	10·1	−2·1	1·8	−0·2	0·11
5	9	9·6	−0·6	1·8	−0·2	0·13
6	15	9·4	5·6	1·7	0·3	0·21
7	11	10·8	0·2	2·1	0·3	0·16
8	10	10·9	−0·9	1·9	0·2	0·11
9	12	10·6	1·4	1·8	0·3	0·18
10	12	11·0	1·0	1·7	0·4	0·23
11	7	11·2	−4·2	1·7	−0·1	0·04
12	10	10·2	−0·2	1·9	−0·1	0·04
13	13	10·1	2·9	1·7	0·2	0·12
14	11	10·9	0·1	1·9	0·2	0·11
15	8	10·9	−2·9	1·7	−0·1	0·06
16	13	10·2	2·8	1·8	0·2	0·11
17	10	10·9	−0·9	1·9	0·1	0·04
18	14	10·7	3·3	1·8	0·4	0·23
19	20	11·5	8·5	2·0	1·2	0·62
20	24	13·6	10·4	2·6	2·1	0·82
21	16	16·2	−0·2	3·4	1·9	0·56
22	17	16·2	0·8	3·1	1·8	0·58
23	20	16·4	3·6	2·9	2·0	0·69
24	19	17·3	1·7	2·9	2·0	0·67
25	22	17·7	4·3	2·8	2·2	0·78
26	20	18·8	1·2	3·0	2·1	0·71
27	21	19·1	1·9	2·8	2·1	0·74
28	17	19·6	−2·6	2·7	1·6	0·60
29	18	18·9	−0·9	2·7	1·4	0·51
30	20	18·7	1·3	2·5	1·4	0·54
31	25	19·0	6·0	2·4	1·8	0·76
32	15	20·5	−5·5	2·7	1·1	0·39
33	20	19·1	0·9	3·0	1·1	0·35
34	21	19·4	1·6	2·8	1·1	0·40
35	22	19·8	2·2	2·7	1·2	0·46
36	21	20·3	0·7	2·6	1·2	0·44

The two sets of results are plotted in Figs. 18 and 19.

It can be seen that the average error for Trigg's method is 2·28, whereas the 'best average α' technique has a result of 2·35, with the advantage of knowing in advance what the best α would be.

Trigg's method is a technique which will provide a stable response after the sales have been level for a short period, and will become sensitive soon after a change in demand level. There is of course a lag in response, because we are only considering past data, but, as can be seen in the example, the response rate is quite rapid.

The forecasting technique developed so far will deal adequately with sales which fluctuate around a given level, and will follow the sales when the demand level changes, indicating that a change has occurred by generating a tracking signal.

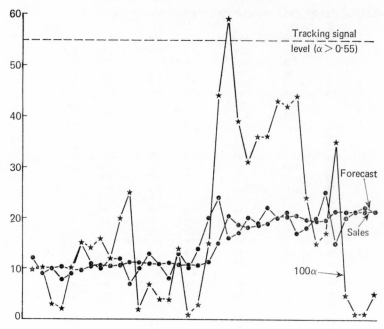

Fig. 18. Sales history 5: Trigg's method

Exponential smoothing methods are quite satisfactory for this kind of data. But it is common for items to show yearly cycles in demand, so that a seasonal pattern of sales is generated. Such regular peaks and valleys in sales tend to be more acute in the retail industry, but less so in wholesale and manufacturing because of the smoothing-

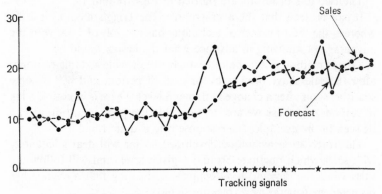

Fig. 19. Sales history 5: exponential smoothing ($\alpha = 0.25$)

out effect of the different lead times and ordering policies of the wholesaler's or manufacturer's customers.

Exponential smoothing operates very badly when demand shows a seasonal cycle. It tends to forecast high when demand is low and vice versa, which is not a very satisfactory thing for a forecasting system to do. Look at the effects produced by exponential smoothing with Trigg's method operating on a seasonal demand pattern:

SALES HISTORY 6: FORECAST BY TRIGG'S METHOD

Period	Sales	Forecast	Error	MAD	SE	α
1	8	11·0	−3·0	12·0	−0·3	0·10
2	6	10·9	−4·9	11·1	−0·8	0·03
3	8	10·6	−2·6	10·5	−0·9	0·07
4	5	10·3	−5·3	9·7	−1·4	0·10
5	15	9·5	5·5	9·3	−0·7	0·15
6	9	9·9	−0·9	8·9	−0·7	0·08
7	7	9·9	−2·9	8·1	−0·9	0·09
8	15	9·5	5·5	7·6	−0·3	0·12
9	17	9·7	7·3	7·4	0·5	0·04
10	55	10·2	44·8	7·3	4·9	0·06
11	39	30·0	9·0	11·1	5·3	0·44
12	21	34·4	−13·4	10·9	3·4	0·49
13	12	30·2	−18·2	11·1	1·3	0·31
14	8	28·3	−20·3	11·8	−0·9	0·11
15	10	26·9	−16·9	12·7	−2·5	0·07
16	10	23·7	−13·7	13·1	−3·6	0·19
17	18	19·9	−1·9	13·2	−3·4	0·27
18	11	19·4	−8·4	12·0	−3·9	0·29
19	9	16·6	−7·6	11·7	−4·3	0·34
20	19	13·7	5·3	11·3	−3·3	0·38
21	40	15·3	24·7	10·7	−0·5	0·31
22	43	16·4	26·6	12·1	2·2	0·04
23	35	20·7	14·3	13·5	3·4	0·16
24	26	24·3	1·7	13·6	3·2	0·25
25	13	24·7	−11·7	12·4	1·7	0·26
26	10	23·1	−13·1	12·3	0·2	0·14
27	12	22·8	−10·8	12·4	−0·9	0·02
28	9	22·1	−13·1	12·3	−2·1	0·07
29	11	19·9	−8·9	12·3	−2·8	0·17
30	15	17·8	−2·8	12·0	−2·8	0·23
31	12	17·1	−5·1	11·1	−3·0	0·25
32	16	15·7	0·3	10·5	−2·7	0·29
33	43	15·8	27·2	9·5	0·3	0·28
34	51	16·5	34·5	11·2	3·7	0·03
35	31	26·0	5·0	13·6	3·9	0·28
36	18	27·6	−9·6	12·7	2·5	0·30

A graph of this example is shown in Fig. 20.

It can be seen very clearly in the example that any exponential smoothing method is likely to produce very large errors with seasonal demand. The forecasts become out of phase with the sales, and high average errors result. In this case the average error was 11·3

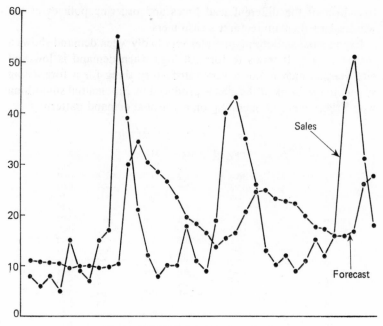

Fig. 20. Sales history 6: Trigg's method

and the average of sales is about 20. The forecast has a 50 per cent error on average, and the resulting forecast in this case would be a statement that the sales are likely to be between 8 and 48 for 90 per cent of the time – which is not very useful.

The first solution to the problem of seasonality was to calculate a monthly average of sales, so as to have some idea of the seasonal pattern, and to superimpose exponential smoothing on this. However, in order to calculate any reliable monthly shape for the sales, it is necessary to have at least two years' actual sales history for use as a basis. This is a feature of nearly all seasonal forecasting systems, and items with less than two years' history available need special, less satisfactory, techniques for estimating their seasonal pattern. If less than two years' history is available, it may be necessary to guess the monthly pattern of sales, assume that the pattern will be the same as for a similar item, work from national statistics, or make do with simple exponential smoothing until the necessary history has accumulated.

This technique will be used for sales history 6, but the first two years will be taken to produce the seasonal pattern, and the forecast will be generated for the third year.

The seasonal pattern is as follows:

Month	1	2	3	4	5	6	7	8	9	10	11	12
Year 1	8	6	8	5	15	9	7	15	17	55	39	21
Year 2	12	8	10	10	18	11	9	19	40	43	35	26
Average	10	7	9	7·5	16·5	10	8	17	28·5	49	37	23·5

We then use exponential smoothing to forecast what the demand will be relative to the seasonal base. For example, if sales in month 1 of year 3 are 10, then the demand ratio is 10/10 or 1·0. If sales in month 1 are 15, then the sales are 150 per cent of normal and the demand ratio will be 1·5.

SALES HISTORY 6: EXPONENTIAL SMOOTHING (TRIGG) WITH BASE SERIES

Period	Sales	Seasonal base	Demand ratio	Forecast	Forecast ratio	Error	MAD	SE	α
25	13	10·0	1·3	10·0	1·00	3·0	4·0	0·30	0·07
26	10	7·0	1·4	7·2	1·02	2·8	3·9	0·55	0·14
27	12	9·0	1·3	9·7	1·08	2·3	3·8	0·73	0·19
28	9	7·5	1·2	8·5	1·13	0·5	3·6	0·71	0·19
29	11	16·5	0·7	18·9	1·14	−7·9	3·3	−0·15	0·04
30	15	10·0	1·5	11·2	1·12	3·8	3·8	0·25	0·06
31	12	8·0	1·5	9·2	1·15	2·8	3·8	0·50	0·13
32	16	17·0	0·9	20·3	1·19	−4·3	3·7	0·03	0·01
33	43	28·5	1·5	34·0	1·19	9·0	3·7	0·93	0·25
34	51	49·0	1·0	62·2	1·27	−11·2	4·3	−0·29	0·07
35	31	37·0	0·8	46·4	1·25	−15·4	5·0	−1·80	0·36
36	18	23·5	0·8	25·9	1·10	−7·9	6·0	−2·41	0·40

These forecasts are plotted in Fig. 21. The average error produced by exponential smoothing with base series is 5·9, much smaller than the 11·3 produced by exponential smoothing alone. Some disadvantages of the method can be seen in the example, however. Firstly, it is necessary to keep a permanent record of the 12 base series values, which increases the record-keeping problem. Secondly, the base series values have to be updated in some way in case there is a change in the seasonal shape (this is normally done with exponential smoothing, using a high α factor). Notice also that the small fluctuations above forecast in periods 25, 26, 30, 31 and 33 cause the peak to be forecast at 62, which is far too high. It would have been preferable in this case simply to use the base series for forecasting, without any smoothing. This would have produced an average error

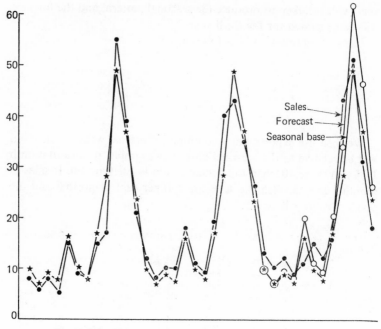

Fig. 21. Sales history 6: exponential smoothing with base series

of 4·5 — considerably better than 5·9. However, smoothing *is* necessary in order to capture changes in demand. The basic objection to the method used in the example is that small fluctuations during low periods of the year are amplified when forecasting sales peaks. This makes the technique very unstable where high peaks and low valleys of demand are likely to occur. Shifts in peak from one month to the next also cause havoc. A more satisfactory solution for seasonal demand is to use R. G. Brown's adaptive forecasting method with a seasonal model. This technique will be described at a later stage, as it is of value in a wide range of situations.

The techniques described so far will operate correctly on demand which changes level, fluctuates around a fixed level, or shows a regular seasonal pattern. They are less satisfactory if the demand shows a consistent uptrend or downtrend. However fast exponential smoothing can be made to follow demand, it can never catch up with a trending item. Here is the process of exponential smoothing carried out on an item which starts at a constant average level of

10 and then develops an uptrend in sales of approximately 2 per month:

SALES HISTORY 7: TRIGG'S METHOD

Period	Sales	Forecast	Error	MAD	SE	α
1	12	10·0	2·0	3·0	0·2	0·10
2	10	10·1	−0·1	2·9	0·2	0·07
3	8	10·1	−2·1	2·6	−0·1	0·06
4	9	10·1	−1·1	2·6	−0·2	0·02
5	11	10·0	1·0	2·4	−0·0	0·07
6	6	10·0	−4·0	2·3	−0·4	0·02
7	13	9·3	3·7	2·5	−0·0	0·18
8	10	9·3	0·7	2·6	0·0	0·01
9	11	9·3	1·7	2·4	0·2	0·02
10	11	9·5	1·5	2·3	0·3	0·09
11	13	9·7	3·3	2·2	0·6	0·15
12	13	10·6	2·4	2·3	0·8	0·27
13	18	11·4	6·6	2·3	1·4	0·34
14	21	14·7	6·3	2·8	1·9	0·50
15	20	18·5	1·5	3·1	1·8	0·60
16	21	19·4	1·6	3·0	1·8	0·62
17	21	20·4	0·6	2·8	1·7	0·64
18	29	20·8	8·2	2·6	2·3	0·65
19	27	26·9	0·1	3·2	2·1	0·74
20	30	27·0	3·0	2·9	2·2	0·74
21	32	29·3	2·7	2·9	2·3	0·77
22	35	31·4	3·6	2·9	2·4	0·79
23	37	34·3	2·7	2·9	2·4	0·82
24	40	36·6	3·4	2·9	2·5	0·83
25	35	39·5	−4·5	3·0	1·8	0·85
26	42	36·9	5·1	3·1	2·1	0·58
27	44	40·2	3·8	3·3	2·3	0·65

The results are plotted in Fig. 22.

It can be seen that the forecast never catches up with the demand, and a very high α factor is produced, which makes the forecast extremely sensitive to minor variations. It is questionable whether violent uptrends or downtrends are maintained for long enough periods in stock control to make it worth while allowing for them in the forecasting method used. The great disadvantage of including a trend component in the forecasting technique is that it is very likely to become unstable. Thus, when there is no significant trend shown by the item, or when the level changes slightly, violent variations in the forecast are likely to occur. However, a simple version of Brown's adaptive forecasting method works very efficiently when a trend occurs, and this method is now shown in operation on sales history 7.

The method of forecasting with trend makes it necessary to recompute a trend each time-period. The trend is added to the 'average' forecast each time-period, before updating takes place.

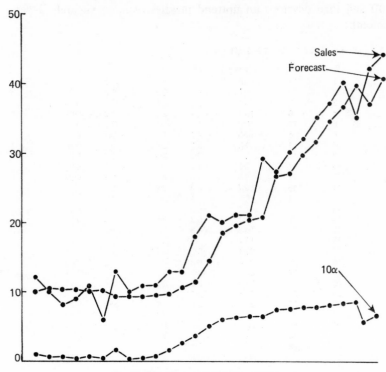

Fig. 22. Sales history 7: Trigg's method

The procedure, using a combination of Brown's and Trigg's methods, is as follows:

1 Compute α factor normally.
2 Current average = old average + old trend.
3 Error = sales − forecast.
4 New average = current average + (α × error).
5 New trend = old trend + (($1 - \sqrt{1 - \alpha})^2$ × error).
6 New forecast = new average + new trend.

The average error on sales history 7 using Trigg's method is 2·9, whereas Brown's method (see opposite) gives 2·1 − a considerable improvement on these data. This method is shown graphically in Fig. 23.

There are older methods of allowing for trends when forecasting, for example 'double exponential smoothing', but these methods are

SALES HISTORY 7: ADAPTIVE FORECASTING (TREND MODEL)
(TRIGG & BROWN)

Period	Sales	Forecast	Error	MAD	SE	α	$(1 - \sqrt{1 - \alpha})$	Average	Trend
1	12	10·0	2·0	3·0	0·20	0·07	0·001232	10·1	0·0025
2	10	10·1	−0·1	2·9	0·17	0·06	0·001030	10·1	0·0023
3	8	10·1	−2·1	2·6	−0·06	0·03	0·000159	10·1	0·0020
4	9	10·1	−1·1	2·6	−0·17	0·07	0·001218	10·0	0·0007
5	11	10·0	1·0	2·4	−0·05	0·02	0·000125	10·0	0·0008
6	6	10·0	−4·0	2·3	−0·45	0·18	0·009199	9·3	−0·0363
7	13	9·2	3·8	2·5	−0·03	0·01	0·000026	9·3	−0·0362
8	10	9·2	0·8	2·6	0·05	0·02	0·000127	9·3	−0·0361
9	11	9·2	1·8	2·4	0·23	0·10	0·002482	9·4	−0·0317
10	11	9·4	1·6	2·3	0·37	0·16	0·007197	9·7	−0·0198
11	13	9·6	3·4	2·3	0·67	0·28	0·023173	10·6	0·0587
12	13	10·7	2·3	2·4	0·83	0·35	0·037715	11·4	0·1453
13	18	11·7	6·3	2·4	1·38	0·50	0·084790	14·7	0·6761
14	21	16·1	4·9	2·8	1·73	0·58	0·124245	18·3	1·2896
15	20	20·8	−0·8	3·0	1·48	0·53	0·100338	19·1	1·2061
16	21	21·5	−0·5	2·8	1·28	0·50	0·086770	20·0	1·1617
17	21	22·4	−1·4	2·5	1·01	0·42	0·056041	20·6	1·0849
18	29	22·8	6·2	2·4	1·53	0·55	0·106479	25·1	1·7443
19	27	28·6	−1·6	2·8	1·22	0·45	0·068270	26·1	1·6355
20	30	29·4	0·6	2·7	1·16	0·47	0·073094	28·0	1·6797
21	32	31·4	0·6	2·5	1·10	0·48	0·078377	30·0	1·7265
22	35	33·5	1·5	2·3	1·14	0·52	0·093284	32·5	1·8698
23	37	36·3	0·7	2·2	1·10	0·53	0·100992	34·8	1·9434
24	40	38·7	1·3	2·1	1·12	0·57	0·116181	37·5	2·0970
25	35	41·7	−6·7	2·0	0·34	0·14	0·005296	38·6	2·0616
26	42	42·8	−0·8	2·5	0·23	0·10	0·002748	40·6	2·0595
27	44	44·7	−0·7	2·3	0·14	0·06	0·001045	42·6	2·0587

generally difficult to explain and produce less stable forecasts than the adaptive forecasting trend model demonstrated above.

It would be possible to combine the most effective methods studied so far and produce a forecasting technique using a base series, the adaptive forecasting trend model, and Trigg's method of determining α. Such a technique would produce good forecasts for data showing random fluctuation around a fixed level, steady uptrends or downtrends, changes in demand level, and/or regular seasonal patterns. A certain amount of instability would be caused by the inclusion of a trend element, and to this would be added the seasonal instability mentioned previously under the base series heading, where small fluctuations in low season are amplified in high season. It is unsatisfactory to treat the average and trend as elements separate from the seasonal pattern. This is what the combined technique would do, first normalizing the seasonal pattern by dividing demand by the monthly base index, then treating the resulting number as an average, and finally reintroducing the seasonality. Errors in either part could amplify each other.

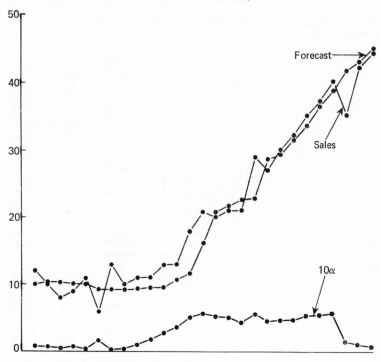

Fig. 23. Sales history 7: adaptive forecasting (trend model)

A far more satisfactory solution for sales forecasting is provided by Brown's adaptive forecasting method, a limited application of which has already been seen in operation, and which will be briefly described here. (For a more detailed treatment of the technique see *Smoothing, Forecasting and Prediction of Discrete Time Series* by R. G. Brown.)

The possible kinds of data pattern treated by Brown's method are quite varied. They include average levels, trends, accelerating trends and higher polynomials, and exponential and trigonometric functions. For the purposes of sales forecasting a limited application of the technique seems indicated. In particular, the elements of the technique dealing with averages, trends and trigonometric functions seem to provide a workable method of forecasting sales data without excessive computation time.

A major advantage of Brown's method is that it treats all elements of the forecast simultaneously, as a continuous whole, rather than piecemeal as in the base series method. The method of dealing with seasonal patterns is very interesting and effective.

Seasonal patterns are sales shapes which recur at regular intervals. Usually the basic interval involved is one year. In dealing mathematically with seasonal patterns it is of advantage to find some formula which has similar characteristics. The sine and cosine functions show the same characteristics as seasonal sales patterns in that they repeat themselves at regular intervals, the difference being that, if the interval is a year, sine and cosine functions repeat them-

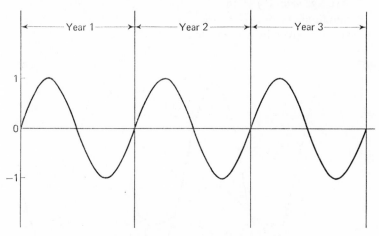

Fig. 24. Basic sine function over three years

selves *exactly* year after year. For example, a graph of the basic sine function drawn over three years is shown in Fig. 24.

Notice that the values fluctuate smoothly between −1 and +1, repeating themselves exactly year after year. If we are to use this function for seasonal forecasting, the first necessity is to make the values reach outside the range −1 to +1. It is very rarely that our sales will be within this area. If the sine is multiplied by a constant factor *a*, the values will fluctuate smoothly between −*a* and +*a*, so that we can reach any numerical sales value that is required. This number we have called *a* is associated with any sine function, and is known as the 'amplitude' of the sine. It is the height of the highest peak (and the lowest valley) that the functions will reach.

The second difficulty is that the values become negative, which will rarely occur with sales. If we combine the seasonal shape of the sine function with the average sales figure x, then x should be greater than a, so that the seasonal pattern will vary between $x - a$ and $x + a$, which is an acceptable pattern. For example, two possible combinations are plotted in Fig. 25:

The next difficulty is that the sine function always has the same shape: a peak in sales one-quarter of the way through the year, and a

1 Average sales $(x) = 10$
   amplitude of sine $(a) = 4$
   shape is given by $x + a$(sine).

2 Average sales $(x) = 18$
   amplitude of sine $(a) = 18$
   shape is given by $x + a$(sine).

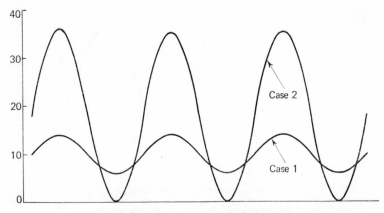

Fig. 25. Sine plus average: two typical cases

valley three-quarters of the way through. There is no problem if the data show only one peak and one valley, in April and October respectively. But if it is otherwise, more flexibility is needed. This is why pairs of functions are always used, a sine function and a matching cosine. The cosine has exactly the same shape as the sine, except that it begins at its highest point, drops, and then climbs again. By combining these two functions, each with its own amplitude, the sales peak can be shifted to any position during the year. Fig. 26 shows two cases, both with average sales of 20 and a total seasonal amplitude of 10. However, the different balance of sine and cosine amplitudes shifts the peak from March in case 1 to June in case 2.

The final difficulty is that, with one pair of functions, the shape is

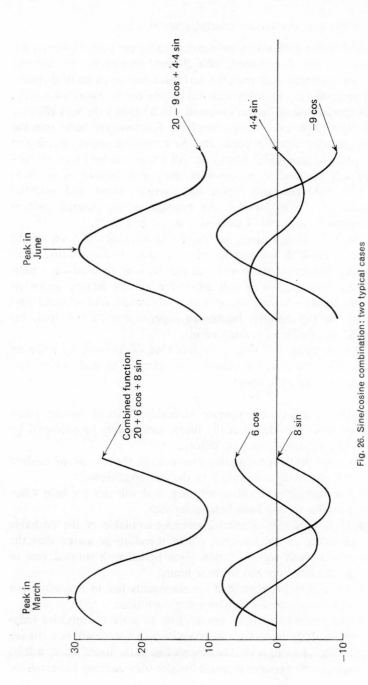

Fig. 26. Sine/cosine combination: two typical cases

limited to one peak *with a symmetrical valley* per year. However, if 6 pairs of functions are used, with different frequencies, so that one pair has two peaks per year, the next three, and so on up to six peaks per year, then *any* monthly seasonal pattern can be described exactly.

A special case of Brown's method which seems to be very effective for sales forecasting is one involving fourteen numbers: one the average sales, one the trend, and the remaining twelve referring to six pairs of sinusoidal functions. All these numbers can be continuously updated by exponential smoothing techniques so as to operate simultaneously upon the average, trend and seasonal aspects of a sales forecast. An example of the possible pattern generated by this sort of method is shown in Fig. 27.

This brief review gives the major characteristics of some of the methods available for making sales forecasts mathematically, based on past history. If these methods can be used to produce a basic routine forecast, which will allow for all the factors which its nature allows — namely changes in level, trends, and seasonal patterns — the merchandise buyer can superimpose on this basis his special knowledge of coming events.

The advantages of producing this kind of forecast, by using an electronic computer, for example, are many. The main points can be summarized as follows:

1 The forecasts will operate smoothly, without human intervention, provided that the future can usually be predicted by extrapolation from past history.

2 Even if the demand pattern does change, the forecasting method will eventually adapt itself to the new conditions.

3 The technique is self-monitoring, and will call for help when the sales show unusual characteristics.

4 There is always a reliable estimate available of the probable accuracy of the forecast; it can therefore be stated that the actual result will be within given limits, with some degree of probability attached to those limits.

5 The techniques described are reasonably fast in operation and will not consume excessive calculation time.

6 The buyer has a basis upon which to place his intuitive judgments. If he decides, for a certain item, that there will be a change in sales, he will probably express this in the form 'There will be about a 50 per cent increase in sales from January to March' or

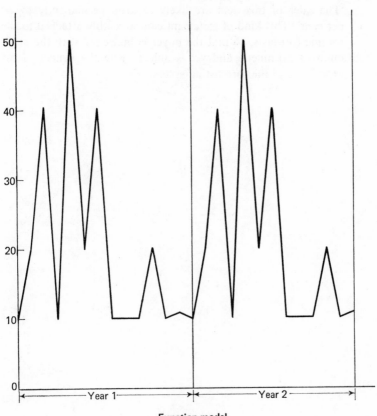

Function model
Average 20
Trend 0

1 peak $\begin{cases} -8\cdot2 \cos \\ 7\cdot9 \sin \end{cases}$ 4 peaks $\begin{cases} -0\cdot6 \cos \\ -1\cdot0 \sin \end{cases}$

2 peaks $\begin{cases} 0\cdot69 \cos \\ -3\cdot6 \; \sin \end{cases}$ 5 peaks $\begin{cases} 6\cdot3 \cos \\ -1\cdot9 \sin \end{cases}$

3 peaks $\begin{cases} -5\cdot7 \cos \\ -1\cdot3 \sin \end{cases}$ 6 peaks $\begin{cases} -2\cdot1 \cos \\ 11\cdot6 \sin \end{cases}$

Fig. 27. Combined effect of six pairs of sinusoids (13 periods per year)

'The sales of this item are likely to drop permanently by 30 per cent'. This kind of statement can be readily attached to the routine forecasts, so that the buyer is burdened with the minimum of arithmetic and yet is able to give the benefit of his experience to the forecasting system.

Chapter 5
Order Quantities

In the previous two chapters, the emphasis has been placed on safety stocks and the calculation of order points. It has been stated that the order quantity affects the safety stock, and in the examples used, a fixed order quantity has been decided upon, and then the order point has been calculated. But as well as affecting the safety stock level, the order quantity also decides the average working stock level. It is sometimes convenient to think of the average stock level of an inventory as being composed of two parts, one of which is the safety stock, the other the cycle stock or working stock. Up to this point the safety stock has been the major consideration, and the factors affecting safety stock can be summarized as follows:

1 Desired level of service.
2 The accuracy of the forecasting method.
3 The lead time.
4 The review time.
5 The order quantity.

In particular, the effect of the order quantity is that a large order quantity causes fewer ordering situations per year, and the safety stock can be lowered to allow greater lost demand in these infrequent order situations. A low order point implies many orders per year, so that the risk of stock-outs will be taken relatively frequently; the safety stock must be raised in order to ensure that the lost sales from any individual order situation are small.

The second, more significant, effect of the order quantity is to raise or lower the working stock level. As stated above, the inventory of an item can be thought of as being composed of two factors, the safety stock and the cycle (or working) stock. The average amount of stock remaining when a delivery arrives is the safety stock. This is because the order point is composed of the forecast for the lead time plus the safety stock. When the lead time has elapsed, i.e. when the order arrives, the remaining stock will be the order point (forecast for lead time plus safety stock) minus sales during the lead time; this, on average, should be equal to the safety stock.

Thus, for a given item, the low point of stock should, on average, be the safety stock, and the highest point which the stock should reach will be immediately after a delivery arrives, when the stock level will be the safety stock plus the quantity delivered, that is, the safety stock plus order quantity. Over a period of time, the average stock holding will be halfway between these two extremes, so that the average stock level will be equal to the safety stock plus half the order quantity.

Historically, in the development of stock-control theory, the effect of the order quantity on the inventory investment was the first to be analysed, as it was very readily seen that the amount of 'cycle stock' or 'working stock' could easily be calculated as half the order quantity. For ease of calculation, the effect of order quantity upon safety stock was ignored, and it was assumed that the working stock could be controlled separately from the safety stock in calculating the inventory policy required. In some cases it is possible to work on this assumption without much loss of efficiency, particularly when the 'optimum' order quantity is very large compared with the demand variability.

For the sake of simplicity, we shall follow the historical development of order quantity theory and ignore the effect of the order quantity on safety stock for the time being.

It has already been shown that there is an annual cost attached to holding stock, made up of capital employed, insurance, maintenance, storage space, deterioration, obsolescence, etc. Suppose that this carrying cost has been discovered, in a particular company, to be about 25 per cent per annum of the average stock value. For the sake of generality we shall use a symbol to represent the carrying cost, and call it r per cent per annum. Ignoring safety stock, what will the working stock of an item cost the company if the order quantity is set at £Q? We know that the average level of working stock is half the order quantity, so the annual cost of working stock under this policy is £$Qr/2$.

In addition to the cost of stock, there is the administrative cost to be considered as well. If the order quantity is £Q and the annual sales value of the item is £S, then the number of orders placed per year will be S/Q.

Now there is some cost involved in making an order. The more orders that are generated, the more staff is required to process the orders; furthermore, many orders mean many deliveries, so that the warehouse staff will have to deal with a larger number of deliveries. In the case of a retail store, deliveries have to be split, price-marked and stored. It is sometimes possible to calculate the cost of making an order. In our example, let us assume that the company in question has calculated that each order costs 5s. to make. It must be remembered that it is somewhat doubtful to attach a fixed cost to each order, as the real costs are a combination of direct order costs and considerations such as 'Do we need an extra man in the warehouse or not?' or 'Do we need another order clerk?' for the increased volume of orders. However, it is often possible to assume that the cost of ordering increases directly in proportion to the number of orders generated. Suppose that this assumption is valid in our example: we have carried out a study and determined that the cost of making an order in this organization is £a per order.

Remember that the number of orders per year generated for a particular item with annual sales of £S and an order quantity of £Q is S/Q.

We can now define the two major costs associated with an order quantity of £Q for this item:

1 The cost of holding stock = £$Qr/2$ per year.
2 The cost of ordering = £aS/Q per year.

Considering these factors in isolation, the total cost associated with an order quantity of £Q is:

$$\text{cost} = Qr/2 + aS/Q.$$

We should like to minimize this total cost. Some numerical examples of the behaviour of these costs may provide an indication of where the point of minimum cost lies.

Item A Annual sales = £2,000. Ordering cost = £0·25 per order. Inventory carrying cost = 30 per cent per annum.

Order quantity	Stock cost	Ordering cost	Total cost
£10	£1·5	£50	£51·5
£20	£3·0	£25	£28·0
£30	£4·5	£17	£21·5
£40	£6·0	£12·5	£18·5
£50	£7·5	£10	£17·5
£60	£9·0	£8·3	£17·3
£70	£10·5	£7	£17·5
£100	£15·0	£5	£20·0
£200	£30·0	£2·5	£32·5

Item B Annual sales = £100. Ordering cost = £0·2 per order.
Inventory carrying cost = 25 per cent per annum.

Order quantity	Stock cost	Ordering cost	Total cost
£1	£0·13	£20	£20·13
£5	£0·6	£4	£4·6
£10	£1·25	£2	£3·25
£20	£2·5	£1	£3·5
£40	£5·0	£0·5	£5·5

Notice how the total cost figure behaves. It is a smooth curve dropping down towards a minimum point which occurs where the stock costs and order costs are very similar. A graph of the total cost figure always shows the same general shape, which is illustrated in Fig. 28.

The point of minimum total cost occurs where the stock-holding cost and the ordering cost are the same. With this fact in mind, it is possible to develop an equation to calculate the optimum order quantity for any item, once we know its annual sales, the carrying cost of inventory per annum, and the cost of making an order.

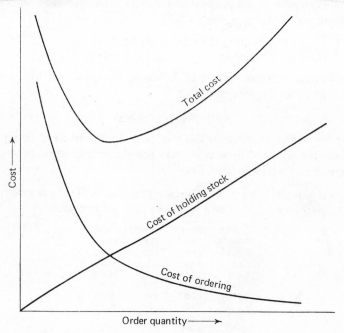

Fig. 28. Economic order quantity curve

The minimum point occurs when the stock costs equal the order costs, i.e.

when $$Qr/2 = aS/Q.$$

We wish to find the optimum order quantity (usually known as the 'economic order quantity', or EOQ). From the above equation we can deduce: $$Q^2 = 2aS/r.$$

Therefore $$\text{EOQ} = \sqrt{\frac{2aS}{r}}.$$

For the two numerical examples given above we can now calculate the EOQ.

Item A   Annual sales = £2,000. Ordering cost = £0.25 per order. Inventory carrying cost = 30 per cent per annum.

$$\text{EOQ} = \sqrt{\frac{2 \times 2,000 \times 0 \cdot 25}{30 \text{ per cent}}} = £57 \cdot 5$$

Item B   Annual sales = £100. Ordering cost = £0.2 per order. Inventory carrying cost = 25 per cent per annum.

$$\text{EOQ} = \sqrt{\frac{2 \times 100 \times 0 \cdot 2}{25 \text{ per cent}}} = £12 \cdot 65.$$

This is another area in which great cost savings can often be made in inventory control. By balancing the work-load costs and the inventory carrying costs correctly, the total cost of an inventory operation can be significantly reduced.

As an aside at this point, some readers may be interested in a mathematical proof of the statement made above that 'the point of minimum cost occurs when the stock-holding cost is equal to the ordering cost'. The proof is as follows:

$$\text{Total cost } (TC) = Qr/2 + aS/Q.$$

We try to vary Q so that TC is at its minimum.

A minimum will occur when $\dfrac{dTC}{dQ} = 0.$

$$\frac{dTC}{dQ} = \frac{r}{2} - \frac{aS}{Q^2}$$

but $$\frac{dTC}{dQ} = 0$$

therefore $$\frac{r}{2} - \frac{aS}{Q^2} = 0$$

so $$Q^2 = 2aS/r \quad \text{or} \quad Q = \sqrt{2aS/r}$$

which is the EOQ formula shown above.

This formula, which was first devised early in this century, has found a wide range of application. The examples shown have been in the area of simple stock control. However, the EOQ formula can also be applied to some kinds of manufacturing process. If a single production line is used to manufacture several distinct products, then there is a certain set-up cost involved in cleaning out the production line and setting it up to manufacture a different product. Therefore it would seem to be economical to have very long runs and incur the unproductive cleaning and set-up process as infrequently as possible. If long runs are made, then large inventories will build up of the product under manufacture. Again we have the problem of costs of short runs (small orders) against costs of large runs (large stocks). The EOQ formula can often be applied to situations of this type, substituting the cost of set-up for the cost of ordering.

There is one major factor which often determines the size of the order quantity in a wholesale or retail environment. This is the price discount offered by the supplier for large orders. The order quantity of the wholesaler will often be determined completely by the discount structure offered to him. By using an EOQ analysis, it is possible to discover whether it is really worth while to increase the order quantity to gain a discount. In this case we have to examine several possible ordering strategies. First we shall consider a simple discount situation where only one discount breakpoint is offered by the supplier. In algebraic terms, let S be the annual sales of the item *in units*, Q the order quantity *in units*, c_1 the normal cost price, c_2 the effective unit-cost price if the discount is achieved, and P the fixed selling price of the item. The carrying cost, r per cent per annum, must be defined as the percentage carrying cost valued at cost price.

There are two possibilities. Firstly, if we order less than the discount breakpoint, then the costs will be:

ordering cost aS/Q
carrying cost $rQc_1/2$

and the most economical strategy under these circumstances will be where

$$aS/Q = rQc_1/2$$

$$Q = \sqrt{\frac{2aS}{rc_1}}.$$

If the order is greater than the discount breakpoint, then the relative costs will be:

ordering costs aS/Q

inventory costs $\dfrac{rQc_2}{2}$

extra profit per annum received $S(c_1 - c_2)$.

The results of these considerations can best be analysed by the use of several examples. Firstly, take an item with the following characteristics:

Annual sales in units 500.
Normal cost price £1.
Cost of making an order 10s.
Inventory carrying cost 25 per cent per annum.
If 500 or more units are ordered in any one order, the cost price drops to 18s. per unit.

The normal EOQ, excluding discounts, gives the following result:

$$Q = \sqrt{\frac{2 \times \cdot 5 \times 500}{\cdot 25 \times 1 \cdot 0}} = 45 \text{ units}$$

and the annual cost of this strategy will be:

ordering costs $= aS/Q = (0 \cdot 5 \times 500)/45 = £5 \cdot 6$
inventory costs $= rQc_1/2 = (45 \times 0 \cdot 25 \times 1)/2 = £5 \cdot 6$
total annual cost $= £11 \cdot 2$.

The EOQ under the discount strategy would be

$$Q = \sqrt{\frac{2 \times \cdot 5 \times 500}{\cdot 25 \times \cdot 9}} = 47 \text{ units}$$

It is impossible to achieve this, as the discount structure starts at an order of 500 units. Therefore the lowest cost strategy in accepting the discount is to order 500, which gives the following costs:

$$\text{ordering cost} = aS/Q = 10\text{s.} = £0\cdot5$$

$$\text{inventory cost} = rQc_2/2 = \frac{500 \times \cdot9 \times \cdot25}{2} = £56\cdot3$$

$$\text{extra profit per year} = S(c_1 - c_2) = 500 \times 2\text{s.} = £50.$$

Therefore the relative cost of taking the discount is

$$£56\cdot3 + £0\cdot5 - £50 \doteqdot £7.$$

This is less than the cost of ordering without the discount (£11·2), so that the correct policy is to order 500 units at a time in order to obtain the discount.

In the above example we have assumed a discount of 10 per cent, which is quite high. If the discount was 5 per cent, then the policy of ordering 500 at a time would have the following costs attached to it:

$$\text{new cost price } c_2 = 19\text{s.}$$
$$\text{ordering cost} = aS/Q = £0\cdot5$$

$$\text{inventory cost} = rQc_2/2 = \frac{500 \times \cdot25 \times \cdot95}{2}$$
$$= £59\cdot4$$

$$\text{extra profit for sales} = S(c_1 - c_2) = £25,$$

so that the total relative cost of taking the discount would be

$$£59\cdot4 + £0\cdot5 - £25 \doteqdot £35.$$

This is far greater than the cost attached to ordering 45 at a time (£11·2), so the correct strategy in this case is to ignore the discount and order 45 units each time.

This method of analysis can be applied to more complex situations where several discount breakpoints exist for different order quantities. The procedure is as follows:

1 Calculate the EOQ for each discount's unit-cost price.
2 Find the nearest point to the EOQ allowed by the quantity limits of the discount.
3 Calculate the inventory cost, ordering cost and annual extra profit associated with each of these order quantities.
4 The smallest total cost point is the optimum strategy.

Here are three examples of this kind of analysis:

Item A Annual sales 5,000 units. Cost of ordering £1 per order.
Inventory carrying cost 16 per cent per annum.
Normal cost price 10s. per unit.
For orders of 500 units or more, a $2\frac{1}{2}$ per cent discount is
offered, giving an effective cost price of 9s. 9d.
For orders of 1,000 units or more, a 5 per cent discount is
offered, giving an effective cost price of 9s. 6d.

Alternative 1 Buy at the normal price.
EOQ $= \sqrt{2aS/cr} = 350$ units
cost of ordering $= aS/Q = £14$
cost of inventory $= Qcr/2 = £14$
total cost $= £28$ per annum.

Alternative 2 Buy at the first discount point.
EOQ $= 356$ units; nearest possible point
at this price is OQ $= 500$ units
cost of ordering $= aS/Q = £10$
cost of inventory $= Qcr/2 = £20$
extra profit per annum $= 5,000 \times 3d. = £63$
total cost $= £10 + £20 - £63 = -£33$.

Alternative 3 Buy at second discount point.
EOQ $= 367$ units; nearest possible point
at this price is OQ $= 1,000$ units
cost of ordering $= £5$
cost of inventory $= £38$
extra profit per annum $= 5,000 \times 6d. = £125$
total cost $= £5 + £38 - £125 = -£82$.

The smallest total cost given by the three alternatives is $-£82$ per
annum, for alternative 3, so that the best strategy is to order 1,000
units at a time for item A.

Item B Annual sales 1,000 units. Cost of ordering £1.
Inventory carrying cost 30 per cent per annum.
Normal cost price £5 per unit.
A discount of 2 per cent is offered for buying 200 units at a time,
giving an effective price of £4 18s.
A discount of 5 per cent is offered for buying 2,000 units at a
time – an effective price of £4 15s.

Alternative 1 Buy at the normal price.

EOQ $= \sqrt{2aS/cr} = 36$ units
ordering cost $= aS/Q = £28$
carrying cost $= Qcr/2 = £27$
total annual cost $= £55$.

Alternative 2 Buy at the first breakpoint.

EOQ $= 37$ units; nearest point at this price is OQ $= 200$ units
ordering cost $= aS/Q = £5$
carrying cost $= Qcr/2 = £147$
extra profit per annum $= 1,000 \times 2s. = £100$
total annual cost $= £5 + £147 - £100 = £52$.

Alternative 3 Buy at the second breakpoint.

EOQ $= 38$ units; nearest point at this price is OQ $= 2,000$ units
cost of ordering is $aS/Q = 10s.$
carrying cost is $Qcr/2 = £1,225$
extra profit per annum $= 1,000 \times 5s. = £250$
total annual cost $= 10s. + £1,225 - £250 = £975$.

The lowest cost alternative is to buy at the first breakpoint, and order 200 at a time. However, this strategy is not much cheaper than ordering 36 units at a time; the decision is very dependent on the accuracy of the cost figures a and r.

Item C Annual sales 500 units. Cost of ordering 10s.

Inventory carrying cost 20 per cent per annum.

The normal cost price is £5.

A discount of 3 per cent is offered for ordering 50 at a time, giving an effective price of £4 17s.

A discount of 6 per cent is offered for ordering 200 units at a time—an effective price of £4 14s.

The company policy has been decided that if this article is purchased at £5, the selling price will be £7; if it is purchased at £4 17s., the selling price will be £6 18s., and if it is purchased at £4 14s., the selling price will be £6 16s. It is expected that annual sales will increase to 510 units if the item is offered at a selling price of £6 18s., and that the annual sales will be 525 units if the price is £6 16s.

Alternative 1. Buy at the normal price.

$$\text{EOQ} = \sqrt{\frac{2 \times 0\cdot5 \times 500}{5 \times 0\cdot2}} = 22 \text{ units}$$

ordering cost $= aS/Q = £11$
inventory cost $= Qcr/2 = £11$
annual profit $= 500(£7 - £5) = £1,000$
annual 'net' profit $= £978$.

Alternative 2. Buy at the first breakpoint.

$$\text{EOQ} = \sqrt{\frac{2 \times 0\cdot5 \times 510}{5 \times 0\cdot97 \times 0\cdot2}} = 22 \text{ units}$$

OQ $= 50$
ordering cost $= aS/Q = £5$
inventory cost $= Qcr/2 = £25$
annual profit $= 510(£6 \text{ 18s.} - £4 \text{ 17s.}) = £1,045$
annual 'net' profit $= £1,014$.

Alternative 3. Buy at the second breakpoint.

$$\text{EOQ} = \sqrt{\frac{2 \times 0\cdot5 \times 525}{5 \times 0\cdot94 \times 0\cdot2}} = 23 \text{ units}$$

OQ $= 200$
ordering cost $= aS/Q = £1$
inventory cost $= Qcr/2 = £94$
annual profit $= 525(£6 \text{ 16s.} - £4 \text{ 14s.})$
$\qquad\qquad = £1,102$
annual 'net' profit $= £1,007$.

The maximum profit strategy is alternative 2.

The calculation of order quantities can be further complicated by the fact that many suppliers offer a total quantity discount for an entire order, which may include several lines of merchandise. A supplier might allow a discount on an order whose value was at least £5,000, and it is immaterial which merchandise is ordered or what mix of lines make up the total order. The general effect of this kind of discount is to make it profitable to order the lines supplied by a particular vendor simultaneously; this will presumably also cut the delivery and receiving costs. Somehow the orders for individual lines must be synchronized to produce large enough joint orders to satisfy the discount, providing that it is in fact worth while to accept the discount. Under the methods of inventory control discussed previously each item is controlled separately, with the result that orders for a particular supplier will be scattered randomly over the year, for each individual line.

This particular problem has to be treated as a whole; that is, both the order point and the order quantity strategy have to be varied in order to achieve the objectives. Firstly, the EOQ formula can be used to decide whether or not it is worth while accepting the discount. The total annual sales in pounds of all the items supplied by the vendor must be used as the annual sales figure in the EOQ formula. The costs are then compared with the sum of the costs of all the individual EOQs, supposing that they were ordered independently. It must be remembered that the total ordering cost is likely to be much higher if the items are ordered independently.

For example, a warehouse buys three lines from a particular manufacturer. These lines are item D, item E and item F. The supplier offers a discount of $2\frac{1}{2}$ per cent if the total order exceeds £1,000 in value. The characteristics of the three items are as follows:

Item D. Cost price £1, annual sales 100 units, selling price £1 5s.

Item E. Cost price £5, annual sales 50 units, selling price £6.

Item F. Cost price 5s., annual sales 500 units, selling price 6s.
The inventory carrying cost is the same for all lines — 25 per cent per annum.
The cost of making an order is 10s., and the cost of each line on the order is 2s.
We can develop the EOQ for joint ordering as follows:
cost of making a joint order is 10s. + (3 × 2s.) = 16s.
Annual sales value (at cost price) for supplier

$$= (100 \times £1) + (50 \times £5) + (500 \times 5s.) = £475$$

$$\text{EOQ} = \sqrt{\frac{2 \times 16s. \times 475}{25 \text{ per cent}}} = £55.$$

This does not reach the discount point, so the order quantity must be £1,000

annual ordering cost $= 8s.$
annual carrying cost $= \cdot 25 \times £500 = £125$
extra annual profit $= 2\frac{1}{2}$ per cent of £475 $= £12$

total cost of discount strategy $= £125 - £12 = £113.$

Individual EOQs

$$Item\ D.\ \sqrt{\frac{2 \times 12s. \times £100}{\cdot 25}} = £22$$

$$Item\ E.\ \sqrt{\frac{2 \times 12s. \times £250}{\cdot 25}} = £35$$

$$Item\ F.\ \sqrt{\frac{2 \times 12s. \times £125}{\cdot 25}} = £25.$$

Ordering costs:
Item D £3
Item E £5
Item F .... £3.
Carrying costs:
Item D £3
Item E £4
Item F .... £3.
Total annual costs............ £21.

A clear case for not accepting the discount, so that these items could be treated independently with no further complications. However, let us examine an example where it is worth while to accept a joint discount:

Item G. Cost price £10, annual sales 200 units, selling price £13.

Item H. Cost price £1, annual sales 500 units, selling price £1 10s.

Item I. Cost price 1s., annual sales 10,000 units, selling price 1s. 3d.

A discount of 8 per cent is offered for orders of £2,000 or more. The cost of holding inventory for all items is 30 per cent per annum. The cost of making an order is £1, plus 10s. for each line on the order.

The EOQ for joint ordering would be:

annual sales = (£10 × 200) + (£1 × 500) + (1s. × 10,000)
= £3,000

cost per order = £1 + (3 × 10s.) = £2½

$$EOQ = \sqrt{\frac{2 \times £2 \cdot 5 \times £3,000}{0 \cdot 3}} = £224.$$

This is not possible, so the nearest point is OQ = £2,000

annual ordering costs would be	£4
annual inventory costs would be	£300
extra profit from discount is	£240
total costs of accepting discount are	£64.

Individual EOQs

Item G	£142
Item H	£71
Item I	£71.
Cost of ordering:	
Item G	£20
Item H	£10
Item I	£10.
Cost of holding stock:	
Item G	£21
Item H	£11
Item I	£11.

Total cost of independent strategy = £83 per annum.

So that it is worth while going for the discount.

For these items, then, we wish to synchronize the orders so as to obtain the discount. This means that the normal concept of an order point for each item no longer applies, because individual order points would cause the orders to occur for individual items at different times. Thus the three items must be treated together for safety stocks and service levels as well as for orders: we must consider the *total stock* situation for all three lines.

We have decided how much to order for these three lines – a total of £2,000 each time. We now have to decide when to order. This cannot be done by a total order point for all the lines; we must instead return to the service level for our ordering rule. Suppose that all the lines must be kept at 95 per cent level of service. The calculations are much simpler if one overall service level is specified for all the lines supplied by the vendor, and this is usually the situation which is preferred by the stock controller. The calculations can be adjusted for varying service levels if required, but for the time being we shall deal with the more common situation where the service level for all lines of a particular supplier is the same.

At any point in time, the amount of stock on hand is analysed to decide whether the resultant overall service level will drop below the specified level if an order is not made at the earliest opportunity. If this is the case, the order will be made; if not, it will be delayed until the next review. Here is the analysis procedure, based on our previous example of items G, H, and I. We know that the annual sales of the items are as follows:

Item G .... 200 units
Item H .... 500 units
Item I .... 10,000 units.

Assume that the lead time from this supplier is one month, and that the monthly MADs of the items are as follows:

Item G .... 15 units
Item H .... 20 units
Item I .... 150 units.

We know that the total order quantity of all three lines must be £2,000. On average, this order will be split between the three lines in proportion to their sales rates. Thus the average order quantity of item G will be:

$$\frac{£2,000 \times £2,000}{£3,000} = £1,333 = 133 \text{ units.}$$

The average order quantity of item H will be:

$$\frac{£2,000 \times £500}{£3,000} = £333 = 333 \text{ units.}$$

The average order quantity of item I will be:

$$\frac{£2,000 \times £500}{£3,000} = £333 = 6,667 \text{ units.}$$

Note that each order quantity is equal to two-thirds of a year's supply for each item, so that they should run out at approximately

A.I.C.T.—8

the same time, although random fluctuations in sales will cause the times to vary to some extent. The average monthly sales of each item are as follows:

Item G .... 17 units
Item H .... 42 units
Item I .... 833 units.

Assuming that the items are reviewed daily, so that no allowance has to be made for review time, suppose that the stock position of each item is as follows:

Item G .... 10 units
Item H .... 50 units
Item I .... 900 units.

Then the safety stocks are at the following levels for each item:

Item G .... −7 units
Item H .... 8 units
Item I .... 67 units.

Now the safety stock is composed of K standard deviations, and the standard deviation is approximately 1·25 MAD; we can therefore calculate the K factor for each item, and also the value of the service function, from the service function table.

Item	Safety stock	Standard deviation	K	Service function
G	−7	19	−0·4	0·58
H	8	25	0·32	0·27
I	67	188	0·4	0·23

It was explained in Chapter 3 that the service function is composed as follows:

service function = order quantity(1 − service)/standard deviation.

Thus, if we know the service function, we can calculate the service level at which each item is operating:

$$\text{service level} = 1 - \frac{\text{service function} \times \text{standard deviation}}{\text{order quantity}}.$$

Therefore the service levels of each item are:

Item	Service level (per cent)

G $\qquad 1 - \dfrac{0\cdot58 \times 19}{133} = 91\cdot7$

H $\qquad 1 - \dfrac{0\cdot27 \times 25}{333} = 98\cdot0$

I $\qquad 1 - \dfrac{0\cdot23 \times 188}{6,667} = 99\cdot7$

and the expected annual lost sales are:

Item G $\quad \cdot083 \times £2,000 = £166$
Item H $\quad \cdot02 \times £500 \quad\; = £10$
Item I $\quad\;\, \cdot003 \times £500 \quad = £2.$
Total annual lost sales value $= £178.$

The annual sales value of all the items is £3,000, and we can calculate the overall service level from the formula:

service level = sales/demand = sales/(sales + lost sales)

so that the overall service is

$$\frac{£3,000}{£3,000 + £178} = 94\cdot4 \text{ per cent.}$$

It can be seen that the overall service level has dropped just below our target of 95 per cent. We shall therefore make an order. If the result of the above calculation had been greater than 95 per cent, the order would have been deferred until the next calculation.

The procedure for deciding whether to order a number of joint items from a supplier is quite tedious, and it is of advantage to avoid doing the calculation too frequently. One way of avoiding this calculation most of the time is to calculate a normal order point for each item in the line, based on the desired level of service; the complex calculation is then entered only when one or more of the lines in the supplier's range has dropped below the individual order point. Of course, if all the lines are above their order point, they will show a service greater than the minimum level; we can therefore be sure that the full calculation would also show a service level greater than the minimum.

The next thing to be decided in this example is how much to order of each individual line. Exactly how will the total order be composed? We have decided that the total value of the order must be £2,000 and we have decided whether or not to order. As we are trying to synchronize the ordering of these items, it would be logical to order them so that they will meet their order points simultaneously, or as nearly so as possible. Thus we have to make sure that each item has enough to cover its order point at 95 per cent service, and then *equalize the time supply* for each item, so that each one has, say, nine months' supply of merchandise.

We need enough merchandise to cover the order points. The order points of each item are as follows:

Item G Service function $= \dfrac{133(1 - \cdot 95)}{19}$

$$= 0\cdot 35$$
$$K = 0\cdot 1$$

order point = forecast for lead time plus K standard deviations

$$= 17 + (0\cdot 1 \times 19) = 19 \text{ units.}$$

Item H Service function $= \dfrac{333(1 - \cdot 95)}{25}$

$$= 0\cdot 67$$
$$K = -1\cdot 2$$

order point $= 42 - (1\cdot 2 \times 25) = 12$ units.

Item I Service function $= \dfrac{6,667(1 - \cdot 95)}{188}$

$$= 1\cdot 8$$
$$K = -3\cdot 0$$

order point $= 833 - (3 \times 188) = 270$ units.

(The safety stocks are negative because of the very large order quantity necessitated by the discount—except for item G which has a very large standard deviation.)

Therefore we must have available at least 19 units of item G (£190) plus 12 units of item H (£12) plus 270 units of item I (£14). By the time the order arrives, the stock position will probably be as follows:

Item	Present stock	Forecast for lead time	Remaining
G	10	17	0
H	50	42	8
I	900	833	67

We have to adjust the order for these remaining quantities, so that we must order

19 units of item G	£190
4 units of item H	£4
203 units of item I	£10
Total	£204

The remaining £1,796 must be shared out between the items so that it will last them the same amount of time.

The monthly sales value of item G is £170
of item H is £42
of item I is £42

so that the £1,796 must be shared out in the ratio

170:42:42 or 4:1:1.

Thus the shares will be as follows:

Item	Already allocated	Remainder	Units	Total Value
G	£190	£1,200	139	£1390
H	£4	£298	302	£302
I	£10	£298	6,160	£308

and the total value of the order comes to £2,000.

This sharing-out of the remainder of the order among the items G, H, and I is an example of 'stock allocation'. This subject is treated in more depth in the next chapter.

Chapter 6
Allocation Theory

It is necessary to carry out an allocation of stock whenever a situation arises where a certain fixed supply of merchandise has to be shared out among a number of different items or a number of different physical locations. At the end of the last chapter a situation arose whereby a fixed amount of stock—£2,000 worth—had to be shared out between three separate items, because the supplier offered an advantageous discount for the total order of these three items. In that case the allocation rule followed was to fill the available stock of each item up to the order point which provided 95 per cent service, and then share the remainder so that each item received an equal time supply of inventory. This is a very simple allocation rule, and it is justified in the case of joint orders because the objective is to synchronize the orders for the items in the joint order as far as possible.

There are many applications of the joint allocation procedure used at the end of Chapter 5. One example which is often quoted is the manufacture of paints. A possible situation in paint manufacture is that there is one large vat in which paint of different colours is mixed and processed. This vat has a fixed capacity, but when it is used to manufacture paint of a particular colour, the paint has to be drawn off and stored in cans of varying sizes. There are warehouse stocks of one-gallon, half-gallon, quart, pint, half-pint and quarter-pint cans. When the paint is manufactured, the total capacity of the vat (say 5,000 gallons) has to be shared out among the different-sized cans. This situation is almost identical with the joint ordering situation. The average usage of each size of can will be known, together with the demand variability. There will be existing stocks of each type of can. Usually a single overall service level can be specified for the entire line. It is important to synchronize the stock levels of the different sizes. The procedures described for joint ordering can be applied to this situation without change.

There are many other situations where this simple allocation procedure is inadequate. In cases where synchronizing of the ordering of the different lines is not an objective, the procedure can become more complex. For example, suppose that a manufacturer has a certain quantity of a product coming out of his factory, and he must distribute the total quantity to his 20 regional depots. In this case the most profitable objective would be either to allocate the merchandise so as to obtain the same level of service throughout all the depots, or to minimize the probable lost sales over all the depots. The same situation may apply in a retail chain store, for example, when there is a limited supply of merchandise available from the manufacturer, and the retailer has to allocate this limited supply in the most profitable manner among his retail outlets, of which there might be several hundred. Again, he will wish to allocate the merchandise so as to maximize service or to minimize lost sales (i.e. to maximize sales).

Let us examine a situation of this kind. Take as an example a retail store with five different outlets. The manufacturer of item J has made only 500 units this week. Generally he delivers merchandise every week, and manages to provide as much as is required, but this week he has had trouble and can only supply a limited quantity. Item J has the following characteristics in each store:

Store number	Weekly sales rate	Weekly MAD	Present stock
1	300	40	10
2	100	25	30
3	100	20	50
4	60	20	10
5	10	10	0

The retailer is anxious to share out the available merchandise so as to maximize his sales. To maximize sales is the same as to minimize lost sales, and it is more convenient to think of the problem in these terms. Let us examine the effect of several possible delivery quantities on each of the stores. We shall start by giving each store enough merchandise to cover the forecast sales, and then examine the payoff involved in sending extra stock to that store (see over).

Notice the following points in the calculation of this table. Firstly, the standard deviation is approximated by calculating it as 1·25 MAD. The lead time is assumed to be virtually zero: this stock is available and about to be delivered. We are looking at the probable

Store	Delivery	Total stock	Safety stock	Standard deviation	K	Service function	Lost sales	Extra sales
1	290	300	0	50	0·00	0·400	20·0	***
1	291	301	1	50	0·02	0·390	19·5	0·5
1	292	302	2	50	0·04	0·379	19·0	0·5
1	293	303	3	50	0·06	0·369	18·5	0·5
1	294	304	4	50	0·08	0·360	18·0	0·5
1	295	305	5	50	0·10	0·351	17·5	0·5
1	296	306	6	50	0·12	0·341	17·0	0·5
1	297	307	7	50	0·14	0·331	16·5	0·5
1	298	308	8	50	0·16	0·321	16·0	0·5
1	299	309	9	50	0·18	0·314	15·6	0·4
1	300	310	10	50	0·20	0·307	15·3	0·3
1	301	311	11	50	0·22	0·299	15·0	0·3
2	70	100	0	30	0·00	0·400	12·0	***
2	71	101	1	30	0·03	0·384	11·5	0·5
2	72	102	2	30	0·07	0·365	11·0	0·5
2	73	103	3	30	0·10	0·351	10·5	0·5
2	74	104	4	30	0·13	0·336	10·0	0·5
2	75	105	5	30	0·17	0·317	9·5	0·5
2	76	106	6	30	0·20	0·307	9·1	0·4
2	77	107	7	30	0·23	0·294	8·7	0·4
2	78	108	8	30	0·27	0·283	8·3	0·4
2	79	109	9	30	0·30	0·267	8·0	0·3
3	50	100	0	25	0·00	0·400	10·0	***
3	51	101	1	25	0·04	0·379	9·5	0·5
3	52	102	2	25	0·08	0·360	9·0	0·5
3	53	103	3	25	0·12	0·341	8·5	0·5
3	54	104	4	25	0·16	0·321	8·0	0·5
3	55	105	5	25	0·20	0·307	7·6	0·4
3	56	106	6	25	0·24	0·290	7·2	0·4
3	57	107	7	25	0·28	0·275	6·9	0·3
3	58	108	8	25	0·32	0·260	6·6	0·3
4	50	60	0	25	0·00	0·400	10·0	***
4	51	61	1	25	0·04	0·380	9·5	0·5
4	52	62	2	25	0·08	0·360	9·0	0·5
4	53	63	3	25	0·12	0·341	8·5	0·5
4	54	64	4	25	0·16	0·321	8·0	0·5
4	55	65	5	25	0·20	0·307	7·6	0·4
4	56	66	6	25	0·24	0·290	7·2	0·4
4	57	67	7	25	0·28	0·275	6·9	0·3
4	58	68	8	25	0·32	0·260	6·6	0·3
5	10	10	0	12	0·00	0·400	4·8	***
5	11	11	1	12	0·08	0·360	4·3	0·5
5	12	12	2	12	0·16	0·321	3·8	0·5
5	13	13	3	12	0·25	0·286	3·4	0·4
5	14	14	4	12	0·33	0·256	3·1	0·3
5	15	15	5	12	0·42	0·224	2·7	0·4

lost sales this week, and we must remember that there is normally a weekly delivery of merchandise, so that the average order quantity (Q) is one week's supply, equal to the average weekly sales.

With this in mind, it is possible to calculate the probable lost sales for any possible delivery situation. The delivery is added to the existing stock to show the total stock situation at the beginning of the week. If the forecast sales (average weekly sales) are subtracted from the total stock, we arrive at the safety stock. The safety stock is equal to K standard deviations, so that K can be calculated as the safety stock divided by the standard deviation. We can then look up the service function, which will be called G, from the service function table.

We are interested in the probable lost sales this week. The sales will be equal to the demand multiplied by the service level. The demand will be equal to the average week's sales, and also equal to the average order quantity (as explained above). Therefore, if we call the level of service P, then the sales can be calculated as follows:

$$\text{sales} = PQ$$

so that the lost sales are $Q - PQ = Q(1 - P)$.
Now we have calculated the service function, G, for the particular situation being studied. It is known that:

$$G = Q(1 - P)/\text{standard deviation.}$$

But the lost sales are $Q(1 - P)$
so that we can write

$$G = \text{lost sales/standard deviation.}$$

Therefore, in this case, we can calculate the lost sales directly from the service function and the standard deviation:

$$\text{lost sales} = \text{standard deviation} \times \text{service function.}$$

The result of a number of possible deliveries is shown in the table in terms of lost sales and the extra lost sales covered by increasing the delivery. In the example, there were 500 units of stock available for delivery. The minimum delivery amounts add up to $(290 + 70 + 50 + 50 + 10) = 470$ units. There are 30 more units of stock to be allocated. It seems logical to send this extra stock to the stores where it is likely to give the most extra sales. The highest number of lost sales recovered in the table by delivering one extra item is 0·5, so that we send enough to supply these stores first, then those with lower figures, and so on.

Lost sales gained per unit:	0·5	0·4	0·3
Store			
1	8	1	
2	5	3	
3	4	2	
4	4	1	
5	2		

This allocates the extra 30 units to where they will do the most good, so that the final situation is as follows:

Store	Weekly sales	MAD	Stock NOW	Delivery	Total stock
1	300	40	10	299	309
2	100	25	30	78	108
3	100	20	50	56	106
4	60	20	10	55	65
5	10	10	0	12	12

Total delivery 500

This technique can be used to analyse any delivery situation where there is a fixed amount of merchandise to be shared out. The two most likely objectives are to maximize either the sales or the unit service level, depending on whether profit or customer service is the overriding objective. It is a very tedious analysis, even when carried out by an electronic computer, but there are short cuts available. In particular, Mr. Roger French of Robson Morrow has developed some very elegant solutions to this problem, making the analysis both practical and economical in terms of the amount of calculation time required.

The example of allocation used above is somewhat unusual in that, with an item having a reasonably large sales rate, it would be normal to distribute the item in large packs rather than in single units. Thus the merchandise might have been pre-packed in cartons of ten, for example, and it is often not worth while breaking these cartons down to units before distributing the goods among the individual stores. If this restriction exists, it often simplifies the

Store	Delivery	Total stock	Safety stock	Standard deviation	K	Service function	Lost sales	Extra sales
1	290	300	0	50	0·00	0·400	20·0	***
1	300	310	10	50	0·20	0·310	15·4	4·6
1	310	320	20	50	0·40	0·230	11·5	3·9
2	70	100	0	30	0·00	0·400	12·0	***
2	80	110	10	30	0·33	0·256	7·7	4·3
2	90	120	20	30	0·67	0·150	4·5	3·2
3	50	100	0	25	0·00	0·400	10·0	***
3	60	110	10	25	0·40	0·230	5·8	4·2
3	70	120	20	25	0·80	0·120	3·0	2·8
4	50	60	0	25	0·00	0·400	10·0	***
4	60	70	10	25	0·40	0·230	5·8	4·2
4	70	80	20	25	0·80	0·120	3·0	2·8
5	10	10	0	10	0·00	0·400	4·8	***
5	20	20	10	10	0·83	0·114	1·4	3·4
5	30	30	20	10	1·67	0·019	0·2	1·2

allocation problem, as there are fewer possible delivery quantities to be considered. The analysis in the example would have appeared as shown if the pack size was ten and split packs were not allowed.

As before, there are 30 extra units (three extra packs) to be shared. These packs would be sent to stores 1, 3 and 4 respectively.

These two analyses provide an opportunity for comparing the costs of lost sales which result if a policy of not splitting packs is used, as opposed to delivering a certain number of units.

CASE 1: UNIT DELIVERIES

Store	Total stock	Safety stock	K	G	Lost sales
1	309	9	0·18	0·314	15·6
2	108	8	0·27	0·283	8·3
3	106	6	0·24	0·290	7·2
4	65	5	0·20	0·307	7·6
5	12	2	0·16	0·321	3·8
				Total lost sales	42·5

CASE 2: FULL PACKS

Store	Total stock	Safety stock	K	G	Lost sales
1	310	10	0·2	0·307	15·3
2	100	0	0·0	0·400	12·0
3	110	10	0·4	0·230	5·7
4	70	10	0·4	0·230	5·7
5	10	0	0·0	0·400	4·8
				Total lost sales	43·5

The cost of not splitting the delivery was only one extra lost sale this week for this item. On the same basis the level of service for split deliveries is 90·9 per cent, and for packs 90·7 per cent.

This difference can become very significant, however, when the pack size is large compared with the average weekly sales, as is often the case in retail.

The problem can become very much more complex when several different types of pack are available: packs may be of different sizes or may contain different mixes of sizes and colours of a single line of merchandise, so that each individual size/colour unit cannot be treated separately. This is a case for a joint ordering scheme coupled with a complex allocation mechanism.

Chapter 7
Some Other Factors Affecting Stock Control Systems

In previous chapters we have thought of a reordering system as a combination of an order point and an order quantity. The order point has defined when to order: when the available stock drops below the order point it is time to order. The order quantity is the amount ordered once the decision to order has been taken. This is by no means the only possible ordering scheme. There are three major possibilities, each of which has its own peculiar advantages and disadvantages. They are the order-point/order-quantity (OP/OQ) system, which we have been using for demonstration purposes; the fixed-interval/order-up-to-level (FI/OUTL) system; and the order-point/order-up-to-level (OP/OUTL) system.

The mechanics of these systems are as follows. The OP/OQ system always orders a fixed amount, the OQ, which is normally determined as an economic order quantity; but it may produce an order at any time, depending upon whether the available stock is above or below the order point at the time of review. The OP/OQ system is a fixed-order-quantity, variable-order-interval system. Strictly speaking, an order is only produced when the stock level is reviewed, so that an order may be placed at any review time.

The FI/OUTL system always orders on a fixed interval; for example, an order might be made every month invariably, but the amount ordered will vary relative to the amount of stock available, the forecast and so on. Every month an order-up-to-level is calculated for each item, and an order is made for each item. The amount ordered is the OUTL minus the available stock. The FI/OUTL system is a variable-order-quantity, fixed-order-interval system.

The OP/OUTL system is a flexible combination of the two previous systems. An order is made only when the available stock falls below the order point, and the amount ordered is the OUTL minus the available stock. This allows for the fact that, at any review time, the available stock may have fallen *well below* the order point. The OP/OUTL system is a variable-order-quantity, variable-order-interval system.

In any particular company, a choice must be made as to the most suitable system of the three. The OP/OQ system is quite similar to the OP/OUTL system in many ways. Normally, the difference between the order point and the order-up-to-level will be equivalent to an economic order quantity, so that, if stock were reviewed very frequently, the orders produced by an OP/OUTL system would be the same as the orders produced by an OP/OQ system. The difference in performance comes when the review time is quite long. In this case it is worth while ordering a little extra in order to top up the stock level if it has fallen significantly below the order point since the last review. Therefore it is simpler to use an order point/order quantity system, and there is very little difference in performance if the review interval is short (a daily review, for example). If the review interval is relatively long compared to the lead time, then the OP/OUTL system is significantly better than the OP/OQ.

For any system, the average order quantity will determine how many orders per year will be generated. If the number of orders per year is very similar to the number of reviews per year, it is worth while considering the FI/OUTL system. It is generally fairly inexpensive to review stock, especially if each sale and receipt is recorded as it occurs, so that there will usually be many more stock reviews per year than orders. However, when a stock-count must be carried out every time a review occurs, then it becomes more expensive to review stock. Under this situation one would like to review stock as infrequently as possible. Once an optimum order quantity is determined, the minimum practical review frequency is to review stock just when the last order could be expected to have been used up, so that the stock will be close to its order point. In this case, one would expect to make an order every time stock was reviewed, so that there is no purpose served by having an order point. Thus a FI/OUTL system will generally be used when the cost of reviewing stock is high, and in particular when stock and sales recording is done by means of recording stock counts and receipts rather than sales and receipts.

It can be seen from the above that the review time is the major factor which determines the kind of ordering system used. The review period also has some disturbing effects on the safety stock. It will be remembered that the normal formula for an order point is as follows:

$$OP = F_{LT} + F_{RT} + SS_{LT+RT}$$

where F stands for the forecast, SS for the safety stock, LT for the lead time, and RT for the review interval. SS_{LT+RT} refers to the safety stock to cover the lead time plus the review time ($= K.1{\cdot}25$ MAD_{LT+RT}). It is not entirely correct to include the full review time in the OP formula. Although at first sight it seems sensible to do this, systems using this rule produced higher stock levels and higher service levels than intended. It was found that too much stock was being carried, and that this extra stock was on average equal to the forecast sales for half a review time: there is $F_{\frac{1}{2}RT}$ extra stock generated. The reason for this can be discovered by examining more closely why the RT was included in the first place. It is obvious that the order point must make allowance for at least the forecast sales during the lead time, or stock-outs will occur regularly. In addition, no orders can be calculated between reviews, so that once it has been decided not to order, there is no further opportunity to order until the next review, and no stock will arrive until at least the review time plus the lead time has elapsed. It is therefore logical to make sure that there is at least enough stock available to cover the forecast sales during the lead time plus review time.

If, at a particular review, the amount of stock held is greater than the forecast for the lead time but less than the forecast for the lead time plus review time, then an order will be placed. However, the amount of safety stock expected is equal to K standard deviations. This figure is determined by the desired service level for the item, and it determines the actual average service level which will be obtained. In fact, the safety stock will sometimes be equal to K standard deviations – if, for example, the amount of stock on hand when the order was placed was equal to the forecast for the lead time plus SS. The safety stock could be equal to K standard deviations plus the forecast for the review time, if the amount of stock on hand when the order was placed was equal to the forecast for the (lead time plus review time) plus SS. On average, the amount of stock left when an order arrives will fluctuate between $K.SD$ and $K.SD + F_{RT}$. This means that the average safety stock on hand when the delivery occurs will not be $K.SD$ as planned, but $K.SD + $

$F_{\frac{1}{2}RT}$. This extra stock is usually called 'early order stock', because it is caused by the order being placed earlier than is strictly necessary. It may be of interest to observe the effect of the OP/OQ system with the full review time operating on some sample data, so as to see how the stock levels and service levels vary from their expected values. The data are as follows:

ORDERING STRATEGY SALES HISTORY (FORECAST= 11, $\alpha = 0$)

Period	Sales	Forecast	Error	MAD	CUSUM	SE
1	15	11	4	1·0	4	0·4
2	11	11	0	1·3	4	0·4
3	10	11	−1	1·2	3	0·2
4	7	11	−4	1·2	−1	−0·2
5	10	11	−1	1·4	−2	−0·3
6	14	11	3	1·4	1	0·0
7	11	11	0	1·6	1	0·0
8	12	11	1	1·4	2	0·1
9	10	11	−1	1·4	1	0·0
10	17	11	6	1·3	7	0·6
11	11	11	0	1·8	7	0·6
12	8	11	−3	1·6	4	0·2
13	9	11	−2	1·8	2	−0·0
14	4	11	−7	1·8	−5	−0·7
15	16	11	5	2·3	0	−0·1
16	9	11	−2	2·6	−2	−0·3
17	6	11	−5	2·5	−7	−0·8
18	15	11	4	2·8	−3	−0·3
19	10	11	−1	2·9	−4	−0·4
20	10	11	−1	2·7	−5	−0·4
21	16	11	5	2·5	0	0·1
22	13	11	2	2·8	2	0·3
23	13	11	2	2·7	4	0·5
24	11	11	0	2·6	4	0·4
25	12	11	1	2·4	5	0·5
26	12	11	1	2·2	6	0·5
27	14	11	3	2·1	9	0·8
28	9	11	−2	2·2	7	0·5
29	11	11	0	2·2	7	0·4
30	8	11	−3	2·0	4	0·1
31	12	11	1	2·1	5	0·2
32	11	11	0	2·0	5	0·2
33	9	11	−2	1·8	3	−0·0
34	14	11	3	1·8	6	0·3
35	5	11	−6	1·9	0	−0·4
36	17	11	6	2·3	6	0·3
37	11	11	0	2·7	6	0·2
38	11	11	0	2·4	6	0·2
39	10	11	−1	2·2	5	0·1
40	14	11	3	2·1	8	0·4
41	6	11	−5	2·2	3	−0·2
42	19	11	8	2·4	11	0·7
43	16	11	5	3·0	16	1·1
44	10	11	−1	3·2	15	0·9
45	13	11	2	3·0	17	1·0
46	11	11	0	2·9	17	0·9

Period	Sales	Forecast	Error	MAD	CUSUM	SE
47	8	11	−3	2·6	14	0·5
48	14	11	3	2·6	17	0·8
49	5	11	−6	2·7	−6	0·1
50	7	11	−4	3·0	−10	−0·3
51	10	11	−1	3·1	−11	−0·4
52	15	11	4	2·9	−7	0·0
53	7	11	−4	3·0	−11	−0·4
54	7	11	−4	3·1	−15	−0·7
55	12	11	1	3·2	−14	−0·6
56	15	11	4	3·0	−10	−0·1
57	10	11	−1	3·1	−11	−0·2
58	8	11	−3	2·9	−14	−0·5
59	10	11	−1	2·9	−15	−0·5
60	6	11	−5	2·7	−20	−1·0
61	13	11	2	2·9	2	−0·7
62	6	11	−5	2·8	−3	−1·1
63	8	11	−3	3·0	−6	−1·3
64	9	11	−2	3·0	−8	−1·4
65	8	11	−3	2·9	−11	−1·5
66	13	11	2	2·9	−9	−1·2
67	8	11	−3	2·9	−12	−1·4
68	13	11	2	2·9	−10	−1·0
69	12	11	1	2·8	−9	−0·8
70	16	11	5	2·6	−4	−0·2
71	13	11	2	2·8	−2	−0·0
72	14	11	3	2·8	1	0·3
73	7	11	−4	2·8	−3	−0·1
74	15	11	4	2·9	1	0·3
75	11	11	0	3·0	1	0·2
76	18	11	7	2·7	8	0·9
77	9	11	−2	3·1	6	0·6
78	11	11	0	3·0	6	0·6
79	11	11	0	2·7	6	0·5
80	10	11	−1	2·5	5	0·4
81	12	11	1	2·3	6	0·4
82	12	11	1	2·2	7	0·5
83	10	11	−1	2·1	6	0·3
84	12	11	1	2·0	7	0·4
85	9	11	−2	1·9	5	0·2
86	7	11	−4	1·9	1	−0·3
87	14	11	3	2·1	4	0·1
88	10	11	−1	2·2	3	−0·0
89	7	11	−4	2·1	−1	−0·4
90	14	11	3	2·3	2	−0·1
91	9	11	−2	2·3	0	−0·3
92	9	11	−2	2·3	−2	−0·5
93	12	11	1	2·3	−1	−0·3
94	13	11	2	2·1	1	−0·1
95	12	11	1	2·1	2	0·0
96	13	11	2	2·0	4	0·2
97	8	11	−3	2·0	1	−0·1
98	11	11	0	2·1	1	−0·1
99	9	11	−2	1·9	−1	−0·3
100	12	11	1	1·9	0	−0·1

In this example, the item being controlled is reviewed every week. The average weekly sales are 11 units. The lead time is two weeks.

The MAD per week is 2·5, so that the forecast for weekly sales can be expressed as 11 ± 2.5. It is assumed that the average sales rate does not change throughout the period of the experiment. The order quantity has been fixed at 33 units; presumably this is an economic order quantity. We can therefore set up the rules to be used to order this item under an OP/OQ system. The order point is defined as follows:

$$OP = F_{LT+RT} + K.SD_{LT+RT}.$$

The lead time plus review time is three weeks.

Assume, for the sake of simplicity, that the lead time is absolutely reliable.

The weekly MAD is 2·5 units, and we are interested in the MAD over a period of three weeks. By the usual extrapolation formula, this is approximately equal to 3·6. The standard deviation is approximately 1·25 MAD, so that the standard deviation over the lead time plus review time will be about 4·5. We know that the order quantity is 33 units, and we might specify a service level of 98 per cent. From this it is possible to calculate the service function:

$$
\begin{aligned}
\text{service function} &= OQ(1 - \text{desired service})/\text{standard deviation} \\
&= (33 \times 0.02)/4.5 \\
&= 0.1467
\end{aligned}
$$

so that the K factor will be found from the service function table to be 0·67.

Thus the safety stock will be 0.67×4.5 ($K.SD$) = 3 units.

The order point, therefore, is the forecast for the lead time plus review time (33 units) plus the safety stock (3 units). Thus we have an order point of 36 and an order quantity of 33 units. This method will be tried out on 100 weeks of sales with the specified average and MAD. The expected average stock level will be the safety stock plus half the order quantity, that is, 19·5 units. The expected sales will be 98 per cent of 1100, or 1078 units, so that we expect to lose 22 sales over the 100-week period. Let us see how these results match with the actual data. The average stock in a given week will be assumed to be the average between the stock at the beginning of the week and the stock at the end of the week.

OP/OQ SYSTEM, OP = 36, OQ = 33

Week	Delivery	Opening stock	Order point	Demand	Closing stock	Average stock	Lost sales
1	0	36	33	15	21	28·5	0
2	0	21	0	11	10	15·5	0
3	33	43	0	10	33	38·0	0
4	0	33	33	7	26	29·5	0
5	0	26	0	10	16	21·0	0
6	33	49	0	14	35	42·0	0
7	0	35	33	11	24	29·5	0
8	0	24	0	12	12	18·0	0
9	33	45	0	10	35	40·0	0
10	0	35	33	17	18	26·5	0
11	0	18	0	11	7	12·5	0
12	33	40	0	8	32	36·0	0
13	0	32	33	9	23	27·5	0
14	0	23	0	4	19	21·0	0
15	33	52	0	16	36	44·0	0
16	0	36	33	9	27	31·5	0
17	0	27	0	6	21	24·0	0
18	33	54	0	15	39	46·5	0
19	0	39	0	10	29	34·0	0
20	0	29	33	10	19	24·0	0
21	0	19	0	16	3	11·0	0
22	33	36	33	13	23	29·5	0
23	0	23	0	13	10	16·5	0
24	33	43	0	11	32	37·5	0
25	0	32	33	12	20	26·0	0
26	0	20	0	12	8	14·0	0
27	33	41	0	14	27	34·0	0
28	0	27	33	9	18	22·5	0
29	0	18	0	11	7	12·5	0
30	33	40	0	8	32	36·0	0
31	0	32	33	12	20	26·0	0
32	0	20	0	11	9	14·5	0
33	33	42	0	9	33	37·5	0
34	0	33	33	14	19	26·0	0
35	0	19	0	5	14	16·5	0
36	33	47	0	17	30	38·5	0
37	0	30	33	11	19	24·5	0
38	0	19	0	11	8	13·5	0
39	33	41	0	10	31	36·0	0
40	0	31	33	14	17	24·0	0
41	0	17	0	6	11	14·0	0
42	33	44	0	19	25	34·5	0
43	0	25	33	16	9	17·0	0
44	0	9	0	10	0	4·5	1
45	33	33	33	13	20	26·5	0
46	0	20	0	11	9	14·5	0
47	33	42	0	8	34	38·0	0
48	0	34	33	14	20	27·0	0
49	0	20	0	5	15	17·5	0
50	33	48	0	7	41	44·5	0
51	0	41	0	10	31	36·0	0
52	0	31	33	15	16	23·5	0
53	0	16	0	7	9	12·5	0
54	33	42	0	7	35	38·5	0
55	0	35	33	12	23	29·0	0
56	0	23	0	15	8	15·5	0

Week	Delivery	Opening stock	Order point	Demand	Closing stock	Average stock	Lost sales
57	33	41	0	10	31	36·0	0
58	0	31	33	8	23	27·0	0
59	0	23	0	10	13	18·0	0
60	33	46	0	6	40	43·0	0
61	0	40	0	13	27	33·5	0
62	0	27	33	6	21	24·0	0
63	0	21	0	8	13	17·0	0
64	33	46	0	9	37	41·5	0
65	0	37	0	8	29	33·0	0
66	0	29	33	13	16	22·5	0
67	0	16	0	8	8	12·0	0
68	33	41	0	13	28	34·5	0
69	0	28	33	12	16	22·0	0
70	0	16	0	16	0	8·0	0
71	33	33	33	13	20	26·5	0
72	0	20	0	14	6	13·0	0
73	33	39	0	7	32	35·5	0
74	0	32	33	15	17	24·5	0
75	0	17	0	11	6	11·5	0
76	33	39	0	18	21	30·0	0
77	0	21	33	9	12	16·5	0
78	0	12	0	11	1	6·5	0
79	33	34	33	11	23	28·5	0
80	0	23	0	10	13	18·0	0
81	33	46	0	12	34	40·0	0
82	0	34	33	12	22	28·0	0
83	0	22	0	10	12	17·0	0
84	33	45	0	12	33	39·0	0
85	0	33	33	9	24	28·5	0
86	0	24	0	7	17	20·5	0
87	33	50	0	14	36	43·0	0
88	0	36	33	10	26	31·0	0
89	0	26	0	7	19	22·5	0
90	33	52	0	14	38	45·0	0
91	0	38	0	9	29	33·5	0
92	0	29	33	9	20	24·5	0
93	0	20	0	12	8	14·0	
94	33	41	0	13	28	34·5	0
95	0	28	33	12	16	22·0	0
96	0	16	0	13	3	9·5	0
97	33	36	33	8	28	32·0	0
98	0	28	0	11	17	22·5	0
99	33	50	0	9	41	45·5	0
100	0	41	0	12	29	35·0	

Notice that only 1 sale was lost in total, giving a service level of 99·9 per cent instead of the specified 98 per cent. The average stock was about 26 units, well above the expected value of 19·5. In fact the excess stock is quite close to the forecast for half the review time (excess stock, $6\frac{1}{2}$ units; forecast for $\frac{1}{2}RT$, $5\frac{1}{2}$ units). This early order stock has caused the service level to be well above the desired level, and has also increased the average stock level. One possible solution to this problem is to drop the order point to compensate, so that the formula for calculating the order point becomes:

$$OP = F_{LT+\frac{1}{2}RT} + K.SD_{LT+RT}.$$

This is not entirely satisfactory either, because the service level then drops below the desired value. This fact will be demonstrated, and then explained. If, in our example, we reduce the order point to allow for the forecast for half the review time, the new order point becomes $36 - 5\frac{1}{2} = 30.5$. Normally one would round this up to 31, but to get as accurate figures as possible, in the example alternate order points of 30 and 31 will be used to simulate the effect of an order of 30·5.

OP/OQ SYSTEM, OP = 30·5, OQ = 33

Week	Delivery	Opening stock	Order point	Order	Demand	Closing stock	Average stock	Lost sales
1	0	36	30	0	15	21	28·5	0
2	0	21	31	33	11	10	15·5	0
3	0	10	31	0	10	0	5·0	0
4	33	33	30	0	7	26	29·5	0
5	0	26	31	33	10	16	21·0	0
6	0	16	31	0	14	2	9·0	0
7	33	35	30	0	11	24	29·5	0
8	0	24	31	33	12	12	18·0	0
9	0	12	31	0	10	2	7·0	0
10	33	35	30	0	17	18	26·5	0
11	0	18	31	33	11	7	12·5	0
12	0	7	31	0	8	0	3·5	1
13	33	33	30	0	9	24	28·5	0
14	0	24	31	33	4	20	22·0	0
15	0	20	31	0	16	4	12·0	0
16	33	37	30	0	9	28	32·5	0
17	0	28	31	33	6	22	25·0	0
18	0	22	31	0	15	7	14·5	0
19	33	40	30	0	10	30	35·0	0
20	0	30	31	33	10	20	25·0	0
21	0	20	31	0	16	4	12·0	0
22	33	37	30	0	13	24	30·5	0
23	0	24	31	33	13	11	17·5	0
24	0	11	31	0	11	0	5·5	0
25	33	33	30	0	12	21	27·0	0
26	0	21	31	33	12	9	15·0	0
27	0	9	31	0	14	0	4·5	5
28	33	33	30	0	9	24	28·5	0
29	0	24	31	33	11	13	18·5	0
30	0	13	31	0	8	5	9·0	0
31	33	38	30	0	12	26	32·0	0
32	0	26	31	33	11	15	20·5	0
33	0	15	31	0	9	6	10·5	0
34	33	39	30	0	14	25	32·0	0
35	0	25	31	33	5	20	22·5	0
36	0	20	31	0	17	3	11·5	0
37	33	36	30	0	11	25	30·5	0
38	0	25	31	33	11	14	19·5	0

Week	Delivery	Opening stock	Order point	Order	Demand	Closing stock	Average stock	Lost sales
39	0	14	31	0	10	4	9·0	0
40	33	37	30	0	14	23	30·0	0
41	0	23	31	33	6	17	20·0	0
42	0	17	31	0	19	0	8·5	2
43	33	33	30	0	16	17	25·0	0
44	0	17	31	33	10	7	12·0	0
45	0	7	31	0	13	0	3·5	6
46	33	33	30	0	11	22	27·5	0
47	0	22	31	33	8	14	18·0	0
48	0	14	31	0	14	0	7·0	0
49	33	33	30	0	5	28	30·5	0
50	0	28	31	33	7	21	24·5	0
51	0	21	31	0	10	11	16·0	0
52	33	44	30	0	15	29	36·5	0
53	0	29	31	33	7	22	25·5	0
54	0	22	31	0	7	15	18·5	0
55	33	48	30	0	12	36	42·0	0
56	0	36	31	0	15	21	28·5	0
57	0	21	30	33	10	11	16·0	0
58	0	11	30	0	8	3	7·0	0
59	33	36	31	0	10	26	31·0	0
60	0	26	30	33	6	20	23·0	0
61	0	20	30	0	13	7	13·5	0
62	33	40	31	0	6	34	37·0	0
63	0	34	30	0	8	26	30·0	0
64	0	26	31	33	9	17	21·5	0
65	0	17	31	0	8	9	13·0	0
66	33	42	30	0	13	29	35·5	0
67	0	29	31	33	8	21	25·0	0
68	0	21	31	0	13	8	14·5	0
69	33	41	30	0	12	29	35·0	0
70	0	29	31	33	16	13	21·0	0
71	0	13	31	0	13	0	6·5	0
72	33	33	30	0	14	19	26·0	0
73	0	19	31	33	7	12	15·5	0
74	0	12	31	0	15	0	6·0	3
75	33	33	30	0	11	22	27·5	0
76	0	22	31	33	18	4	13·0	0
77	0	4	31	0	9	0	2·0	5
78	33	33	30	0	11	22	27·5	0
79	0	22	31	33	11	11	16·5	0
80	0	11	31	0	10	1	6·0	0
81	33	34	30	0	12	22	28·0	0
82	0	22	31	33	12	10	16·0	0
83	0	10	31	0	10	0	5·0	0
84	33	33	30	0	12	21	27·0	0
85	0	21	31	33	9	12	16·5	0
86	0	12	31	0	7	5	8·5	0
87	33	38	30	0	14	24	31·0	0
88	0	24	31	33	10	14	19·0	0
89	0	14	31	0	7	7	10·5	0
90	33	40	30	0	14	26	33·0	0
91	0	26	31	33	9	17	21·5	0
92	0	17	31	0	9	8	12·5	0
93	33	41	30	0	12	29	35·0	0
94	0	29	31	33	13	16	22·5	0
95	0	16	31	0	12	4	10·0	0

Week	Delivery	Opening stock	Order point	Order	Demand	Closing stock	Average stock	Lost sales
96	33	37	30	0	13	24	30·5	0
97	0	24	31	33	8	16	20·0	0
98	0	16	31	0	11	5	10·5	0
99	33	38	30	0	9	29	33·5	0
100	0	29	31	33	12	17	23·0	0

The lost sales in this example were 22, giving a service level of $1078/1100 = 98\cdot0$ per cent, which is the desired level. The average stock level is 20·1, slightly higher than the theoretical result of 19·5. The imbalance of service against stock — service accurate, stock slightly high — may be caused by the fact that there is an even spread of probability that the stock level will be between the forecast for the lead time (plus SS) and the forecast for the lead time plus review time (plus SS) when an order is created. However, the meaning of this variation in terms of safety stock is by no means an even spread: if the stock on hand drops 3 units below the order point (which is quite likely under this system), then all the safety stock has already been absorbed, and the on-hand stock could well be $5\frac{1}{2}$ units below the order point, so that lost sales were more probable than not. Some of these difficulties can be corrected by the use of an OP/OUTL system instead of an OP/OQ system, although this is not necessarily the best answer. The formula for the OP would be the same, but the OUTL would be calculated from the formula below:

$$\text{OUTL} = \text{OP} + \text{OQ} - F_{\frac{1}{2}RT}.$$

In each case the amount ordered would be stock on hand subtracted from the OUTL. The use of this method generates some improvement without much extra calculation, as is shown below. A better solution is to use specified delivery dates, as will be explained later.

In the sample situation we have been using, the order point will be 30·5, as before, and the OUTL will be the OP + OQ $- F_{\frac{1}{2}RT}$

$$= 30\cdot5 + 33 - 5\cdot5$$
$$= 58.$$

An order point alternating between 30 and 31 will again be used to simulate the effect of an order point of 30·5 (pp. 125-6).

The lost sales using an OP/OUTL system are 20, giving a service level of $1080/1100 = 98\cdot2$ per cent. Further, this service level was obtained for a stock of 20·7 units — quite near the target level, and not much more than the OP/OQ system. The fact that the OP/OUTL system performs better than the OP/OQ system in this example is not

OP/OUTL SYSTEM, OP = 30·5, OUTL = 58

Week	Delivery	Opening stock	Order point	Order	Demand	Closing stock	Average stock	Lost sales
1	0	36	30	0	15	21	28·5	0
2	0	21	31	37	11	10	15·5	0
3	0	10	31	0	10	0	5·0	0
4	37	37	30	0	7	30	33·5	0
5	0	30	31	28	10	20	25·0	0
6	0	20	31	0	14	6	13·0	0
7	28	34	30	0	11	23	28·5	0
8	0	23	31	35	12	11	17·0	0
9	0	11	31	0	10	1	6·0	0
10	35	36	30	0	17	19	27·5	0
11	0	19	31	39	11	8	13·5	0
12	0	8	31	0	8	0	4·0	0
13	39	39	30	0	9	30	34·5	0
14	0	30	31	28	4	26	28·0	0
15	0	26	31	0	16	10	18·0	0
16	28	38	30	0	9	29	33·5	0
17	0	29	31	29	6	23	26·0	0
18	0	23	31	0	15	8	15·5	0
19	29	37	30	0	10	27	32·0	0
20	0	27	31	31	10	17	22·0	0
21	0	17	31	0	16	1	9·0	0
22	31	32	30	0	13	19	25·5	0
23	0	19	31	39	13	6	12·5	0
24	0	6	31	0	11	0	3·0	5
25	39	39	30	0	12	27	33·0	0
26	0	27	31	31	12	15	21·0	0
27	0	15	31	0	14	1	8·0	0
28	31	32	30	0	9	23	27·5	0
29	0	23	31	35	11	12	17·5	0
30	0	12	31	0	8	4	8·0	0
31	35	39	30	0	12	27	33·0	0
32	0	27	31	31	11	16	21·5	0
33	0	16	31	0	9	7	11·5	0
34	31	38	30	0	14	24	31·0	0
35	0	24	31	34	5	19	21·5	0
36	0	19	31	0	17	2	10·5	0
37	34	36	30	0	11	25	30·5	0
38	0	25	31	33	11	14	19·5	0
39	0	14	31	0	10	4	9·0	0
40	33	37	30	0	14	23	30·0	0
41	0	23	31	35	6	17	20·0	0
42	0	17	31	0	19	0	8·5	2
43	35	35	30	0	16	19	27·0	0
44	0	19	31	39	10	9	14·0	0
45	0	9	31	0	13	0	4·5	4
46	39	39	30	0	11	28	33·5	0
47	0	28	31	30	8	20	24·0	0
48	0	20	31	0	14	6	13·0	0
49	30	36	30	0	5	31	33·5	0
50	0	31	31	27	7	24	27·5	0
51	0	24	31	0	10	14	19·0	0
52	27	41	30	0	15	26	33·5	0
53	0	26	31	32	7	19	22·5	0
54	0	19	31	0	7	12	15·5	0
55	32	44	30	0	12	32	38·0	0
56	0	32	31	0	15	17	24·5	0

Week	Delivery	Opening stock	Order point	Order	Demand	Closing stock	Average stock	Lost sales
57	0	17	30	41	10	7	12·0	0
58	0	7	30	0	8	0	3·5	1
59	41	41	31	0	10	31	36·0	0
60	0	31	30	0	6	25	28·0	0
61	0	25	31	33	13	12	18·5	0
62	0	12	31	0	6	6	9·0	0
63	33	39	30	0	8	31	35·0	0
64	0	31	31	27	9	22	26·5	0
65	0	22	31	0	8	14	18·0	0
66	27	41	30	0	13	28	34·5	0
67	0	28	31	30	8	20	24·0	0
68	0	20	31	0	13	7	13·5	0
69	30	37	30	0	12	25	31·0	0
70	0	25	31	33	16	9	17·0	0
71	0	9	31	0	13	0	4·5	4
72	33	33	30	0	14	19	26·0	0
73	0	19	31	39	7	12	15·5	0
74	0	12	31	0	15	0	6·0	3
75	39	39	30	0	11	28	33·5	0
76	0	28	31	30	18	10	19·0	0
77	0	10	31	0	9	1	5·5	0
78	30	31	30	0	11	20	25·5	0
79	0	20	31	38	11	9	14·5	0
80	0	9	31	0	10	0	4·5	1
81	38	38	30	0	12	26	32·0	0
82	0	26	31	32	12	14	20·0	0
83	0	14	31	0	10	4	9·0	0
84	32	36	30	0	12	24	30·0	0
85	0	24	31	34	9	15	19·5	0
86	0	15	31	0	7	8	11·5	0
87	34	42	30	0	14	28	35·0	0
88	0	28	31	30	10	18	23·0	0
89	0	18	31	0	7	11	14·5	0
90	30	41	30	0	14	27	34·0	0
91	0	27	31	31	9	18	22·5	0
92	0	18	31	0	9	9	13·5	0
93	31	40	30	0	12	28	34·0	0
94	0	28	31	30	13	15	21·5	0
95	0	15	31	0	12	3	9·0	0
96	30	33	30	0	13	20	26·5	0
97	0	20	31	38	8	12	16·0	0
98	0	12	31	0	11	1	6·5	0
99	38	39	30	0	9	30	34·5	0
100	0	30	31	28	12	18	24·0	0

surprising; the OP/OUTL system is theoretically better when the review time is a significant fraction of the lead time, as explained previously. It should be noted, however, that the order quantities generated in the last example, although they fluctuate around the economic order quantity, are not always exactly equal to it. This is a small disadvantage, as the *frequency* of ordering is more important, from the cost point of view, than the total amount ordered. A quite complex modification to the OP/OQ system will cause it to perform much better in this situation. What is necessary is to calculate the difference between the $F_{LT} + SS$ and the on-hand stock when intending to place an order; an order should be generated whenever the on-hand stock (OH) is less than the $F_{LT+RT} + SS$. The amount $OH - F_{LT} - SS$ is the extra 'early order stock', and this can be avoided by working out how many days' supply this stock represents and adding that number of days to the lead time, either by delaying the order, or preferably by specifying the delivery date. This has the advantage that suppliers get between 0 and RT extra days' notice over their normal lead time, provided that they can be trusted not to deliver early when the opportunity is given. The technique of specifying delivery dates is often rejected because of the complications involved in order writing and control or because it can clash with unloading schedules or suppliers' set delivery schedules. It is certainly worth considering, as it avoids early-order stock anomalies very efficiently.

It may be of interest to see the third ordering strategy operating on the sample data—the FI/OUTL system. This would be set to produce orders every third week without fail, and reviews would only occur every three weeks. Thus the RT is three weeks, not one week. The formula for the OUTL in this system is OUTL $= F_{LT+RT} + K.SD_{LT+RT}$. The weekly MAD is 2·5, so that the five-week MAD is about $\sqrt{5} \times 2\cdot5 = 5\cdot6$, and the five-week SD about 7·0. The service function is therefore $33(1 - \cdot98)/7 = \cdot0943$, and the K factor 0·93. The safety stock is then $0\cdot93 \times 7\cdot0 = 6\cdot5$ units. The F_{LT+RT} is a five-week forecast, or 55 units.

The total order-up-to-level is therefore 61·5 units, which will be considered as 61 units for the example.

FI/OUTL SYSTEM, FI = 3 WEEKS, OUTL = 61

Week	Delivery	Opening stock	Order	Demand	Closing stock	Average stock	Lost sales
1	0	36	25	15	21	28·5	0
2	0	21	0	11	10	15·5	0
3	25	35	0	10	25	30·0	0
4	0	25	36	7	18	21·5	0
5	0	18	0	10	8	13·0	0
6	36	44	0	14	30	37·0	0
7	0	30	31	11	19	24·5	0
8	0	19	0	12	7	13·0	0
9	31	38	0	10	28	33·0	0
10	0	28	33	17	11	19·5	0
11	0	11	0	11	0	5·5	0
12	33	33	0	8	25	29·0	0

Week	Delivery	Opening stock	Order	Demand	Closing stock	Average stock	Lost sales
13	0	25	36	9	16	20·5	0
14	0	16	0	4	12	14·0	0
15	36	48	0	16	32	40·0	0
16	0	32	29	9	23	27·5	0
17	0	23	0	6	17	20·0	0
18	29	46	0	15	31	38·5	0
19	0	31	30	10	21	26·0	0
20	0	21	0	10	11	16·0	0
21	30	41	0	16	25	33·0	0
22	0	25	36	13	12	18·5	0
23	0	12	0	13	0	6·0	1
24	36	36	0	11	25	30·5	0
25	0	25	36	12	13	19·0	0
26	0	13	0	12	1	7·0	0
27	36	37	0	14	23	30·0	0
28	0	23	38	9	14	18·5	0
29	0	14	0	11	3	8·5	0
30	38	41	0	8	33	37·0	0
31	0	33	28	12	21	27·0	0
32	0	21	0	11	10	15.5	0
33	28	38	0	9	29	33·5	0
34	0	29	32	14	15	22·0	0
35	0	15	0	5	10	12·5	0
36	32	42	0	17	25	33·5	0
37	0	25	36	11	14	19·5	0
38	0	14	0	11	3	8·5	0
39	36	39	0	10	29	34·0	0
40	0	29	32	14	15	22·0	0
41	0	15	0	6	9	12·0	0
42	32	41	0	19	22	31·5	0
43	0	22	39	16	6	14·0	0
44	0	6	0	10	0	3·0	4
45	39	39	0	13	26	32·5	0
46	0	26	35	11	15	20·5	0
47	0	15	0	8	7	11·0	0
48	35	42	0	14	28	35·0	0
49	0	28	33	5	23	25·5	0
50	0	23	0	7	16	19·5	0
51	33	49	0	10	39	44·0	0
52	0	39	22	15	24	31·5	0
53	0	24	0	7	17	20·5	0
54	22	39	0	7	32	35·5	0
55	0	32	29	12	20	26·0	0
56	0	20	0	15	5	12·5	0
57	29	34	0	10	24	29·0	0
58	0	24	37	8	16	20·0	0
59	0	16	0	10	6	11·0	0
60	37	43	0	6	37	40·0	0
61	0	37	24	13	24	30·5	0
62	0	24	0	6	18	21·0	0
63	24	42	0	8	34	38·0	0
64	0	34	27	9	25	29·5	0
65	0	25	0	8	17	21·0	0
66	27	44	0	13	31	37·5	0
67	0	31	30	8	23	27·0	0
68	0	23	0	13	10	16·5	0
69	30	40	0	12	28	34·0	0

Week	Delivery	Opening stock	Order	Demand	Closing stock	Average sales	Lost sales
70	0	28	33	16	12	20·0	0
71	0	12	0	13	0	6·0	1
72	33	33	0	14	19	26·0	0
73	0	19	42	7	12	15·5	0
74	0	12	0	15	0	6·0	3
75	42	42	0	11	31	36·5	0
76	0	31	30	18	13	22·0	0
77	0	13	0	9	4	8·5	0
78	30	34	0	11	23	28·5	0
79	0	23	38	11	12	17·5	0
80	0	12	0	10	2	7·0	0
81	38	40	0	12	28	34·0	0
82	0	28	33	12	16	22·0	0
83	0	16	0	10	6	11·0	0
84	33	39	0	12	27	33·0	0
85	0	27	34	9	18	22·5	0
86	0	18	0	7	11	14·5	0
87	34	45	0	14	31	38·0	0
88	0	31	30	10	21	26·0	0
89	0	21	0	7	14	17·5	0
90	30	44	0	14	30	37·0	0
91	0	30	31	9	21	25·5	0
92	0	21	0	9	12	16·5	0
93	31	43	0	12	31	37·0	0
94	0	31	30	13	18	24·5	0
95	0	18	0	12	6	12·0	0
96	30	36	0	13	23	29·5	0
97	0	23	38	8	15	19·0	0
98	0	15	0	11	4	9·5	0
99	38	42	0	9	33	37·5	0
100	0	33	28	12	21	27·0	0

The number of lost sales under the FI/OUTL system is 9, giving an effective service level of 1091/1100 = 99·2 per cent – higher than planned. The penalty paid for reviewing only one-third as often as the other systems is extra stock, and the average stock level in the example was 23·3 units; this agrees quite well with the theoretical value, which would be $\frac{1}{2}OQ + SS = 16·5 + 6·5 = 23$ units. The benefits of reviewing less often are smaller reviewing costs per annum, which can be significant, particularly if the information capture is by regular stock-counts rather than by recording sales as they occur.

The table below summarizes the results of the four experiments.

	OP/OQ full RT	OP/OQ $\frac{1}{3}RT$	OP/OUTL	FI/OUTL
Desired service (per cent)	98	98	98	98
Lead time (weeks)	2	2	2	2
Review time (weeks)	1	1	1	3
Average OQ specified	33	33	33	33
Service level achieved (per cent)	99·9	98·0	98·2	99·2
Expected average stock	25	19·5	19·5	23·0
Average stock achieved	26·5	20·1	20·7	23·3

One disturbing factor which was not taken into account for the FI/OUTL system is that it should have been subjected to a maximum order quantity of 36, as back-orders were not allowed in the example. Any demand greater than the on-hand stock in the example was assumed to be lost sales, rather than back-orders to be delivered when a new supply arrived. Under these circumstances the FI/OUTL system should be limited to a maximum order quantity which is equal to the $F_{RT} + SS_{RT} = F_{3wks} + K.1 \cdot 25 MAD_{3wks} = 33 + 3 = 36$ units. The lack of this limitation caused some of the excess service and stock achieved in the example. The reason for the limitation is as follows: under a fixed-interval/order-up-to-level system, the amount ordered should be designed to produce the result that the amount of available stock (on hand plus on order) at the time of the next review should be equal to the forecast for the lead time plus the safety stock for the lead time. This means that, at the next ordering opportunity, the available stock should be equal to the maximum likely demand during the lead time. Therefore the OUTL is composed firstly of the $F_{LT} + SS_{LT}$ plus an allowance for the fact that one review time will elapse before this stock level should be reached. In order to ensure that there is a high probability that at least $F_{LT} + SS_{LT}$ will be in stock at the next review, the maximum likely sales during the next review time must also be allowed for. These sales are, or course, $F_{RT} + SS_{RT}$. We can therefore define the amount ordered as the order-up-to-level minus the available stock, or $F_{RT} + F_{LT} + SS_{RT} + SS_{LT} - OH - OO$, assuming, for the sake of simplicity, that the OO (on order) is zero. It should be noted that the safety stock figure should really be SS_{LT+RT}, which will be less than $SS_{LT} + SS_{RT}$, and that the total safety stock should be shared out between the lead time and review time in proportion. This system works satisfactorily unless sales have been unusually high, and the stock on hand is very low when a review occurs, especially if it is less than the F_{LT}. When $OH < F_{LT}$ and no back-orders are allowed, then the amount of stock remaining at the next review will be too high if the normal ordering rules are followed. The amount of stock remaining at the next review will normally be $F_{LT} + F_{RT} + SS_{LT+RT} - OH -$ the sales during the RT. When the OH is less than the F_{LT}, the maximum sales during the lead time are the OH. The remaining stock at the next review will therefore be

$$F_{LT} + F_{RT} + SS_{LT+RT} - OH - (OH + \text{sales during } RT - LT)$$
$$= F_{LT} + F_{RT} + SS_{LT+RT} - \text{sales}_{RT-LT}, \text{ and the sales during the}$$

review time minus lead time are likely to be considerably less than the F_{RT}, so that excess stock is generated. If, however, the maximum order quantity is defined as the $F_{RT} + SS_{RT}$, then the remaining stock in the situation where $OH < F_{LT}$ at a review will be $F_{RT} + SS_{RT} - \text{sales}_{RT-LT}$, which should be approximately equal to the $F_{LT} + SS_{LT}$ (the desired remaining stock level).

There are several factors which must be considered if the economic order quantity formula is to be used to determine order quantities. The first and most obvious factor is the pack size. If an item is only delivered in packs of 12, for example, any EOQ which suggests that smaller order quantities than 12 should be used must be overridden, both when the order is generated *and* in the calculation of the service function formula. Secondly, the order quantity must never be less than the F_{RT} on average. This sounds very obvious, but systems designers have been known to make this error. It must be remembered that the OQ figure used in the service function formula must be equal to or greater than the F_{RT}, and also equal to or greater than the *PS* (pack size).

The calculation of economic order quantities for seasonal lines can become suspect. The work-load cost attached to a certain order quantity depends on the number of orders generated per year. Thus, if the annual sales are £S per annum, and the order quantity being considered is £Q, then the average number of orders per year will be S/Q. This is true of seasonal lines also, but the orders will not be evenly spaced throughout the year. More importantly, the average stock level ($Q/2$) may be inaccurate for a seasonal line if the seasonal peak is very acute. Furthermore, it is possible that a seasonal line may meet with one of the OQ limitations during low season. Normally, the order quantity of a seasonal line is expressed in terms of a certain number of weeks' supply. For example, if the annual sales are 500 and the order quantity is 50, the ordering rule will be made that five weeks' supply of this item will be ordered when it is decided to make an order—which will cause a fairly even spread of the ten annual orders throughout the year. In the case of this seasonal line, the order quantity would be the forecast sales for the five weeks starting at the end of the lead time. The order quantity used in the service function formula could be the average OQ or it could be the OQ which would be used this time, depending on how the seasonality of the line affects the MAD—whether there are larger forecast errors in high season than in periods of low demand. There is considerable argument as to whether items do or do not, in general, have higher MADs in season or out of season.

The final area where caution must be observed when using economic order quantities is when the MAD is significantly large compared to the OQ. Under these circumstances it is quite possible that the amount of stock saved by reducing the OQ to a smaller value may be outweighed or very much reduced by the corresponding increase in safety stock. It is possible to use a modified EOQ formula which will take this effect into account.

Chapter 8
Setting Service Levels and Other Parameters

If a company has decided to make a considerable investment of time and money in installing an automatic inventory control system, it will want to see the maximum results from this investment. In the previous chapters many inventory control techniques have been described whose primary purpose is to reduce cost or to increase profit, but these techniques must work within the restrictions and objectives set by the company using them. An inventory system is a combination of conflicting objectives, and in many cases a balance must be struck between lowering costs in one area of operations, only to find that the costs have increased in another area, so that the total system is less profitable than before. One simple example of this kind of cost balancing has been shown in the economic order quantity formula, although this is a simplified formula which does not take into account enough different factors.

There are many areas in inventory control where there are conflicting cost objectives. For example, if the service level is increased, the sales will increase also, which should bring in extra profit; but the increase in service level implies an increased cost of safety stock, and the company must set a service level which balances these two objectives. Money can be saved by using a very simple forecasting system, but this will imply less accurate forecasts, very much larger safety stocks, and a larger cost of holding inventory. A smaller order quantity may be used, which will reduce the average stock holding, but this will imply a larger cost of work-load in order generation and receiving and the marking and storing of merchandise, and an increased safety stock. Stock reviews can be made less frequently, but this will imply a greater safety stock and greater complexity in the ordering calculations.

The two major factors which must be set as objectives for an inventory control system are the desired service level and the order quantity of each item. Normally the service level is set for a group of items together, to reduce the work-load in calculating service levels. The results of the policy chosen can be estimated from sample history information or tried out in practice, and the service level of the group or of particular items within the group modified according to experience. Once the basic costs are defined, it is possible to calculate the most profitable service level for each item, but the formula for doing this is complex, and outside the scope of this book. Some of the major variables affecting the optimum service level of an item are set out below, together with their effect on the service level:

Factor	General effect
Large MAD	} Lowers optimum service level
Long lead time	
Large demand	
High mark-on	} Raises optimum service level
Large order quantity	
High carrying cost of stock	Lowers optimum service level

The order quantity is usually set at the economic order quantity. The usual EOQ formula can be made more accurate by the addition of an extra factor, and a fair approximation to the ideal order quantity which includes much of the effect of safety stock is

$$OQ = \sqrt{2As/r} + SD$$

where SD stands for the standard deviation of forecast errors over the lead time plus review time.

Chapter 9
The Control of Fashion Merchandise

The theories of inventory control explained in the preceding chapters of this book cannot be applied to fashion goods. The special situation of fashion buying demands a completely different approach. Let us examine the fashion environment from the point of view of the buyer.

It is normal to divide the sales of fashion goods into several seasons throughout the year. Each selling season will be unique in the range of merchandise sold by a particular department in a retail store, and it will generally be very different from the corresponding season in preceding years. For example, the sales of a dress department might be divided into four seasons: spring, summer, autumn and winter styles. Each of these styles will involve a different merchandise range and probably a different colour emphasis in each season. This brings out some of the priorities of fashion merchandising: the selling life of a particular style of dress will be confined at most to one selling season, and it may be considerably less than a season. Therefore, when a fashion buyer orders a particular style, he must plan on making the majority of his sales within a very limited time-period—say between eight and thirty weeks—before the style becomes obsolete and there is very little further demand for the stock. He will never have stocked this particular style before, and will have no past information about the sales of the style to guide him. The most significant characteristic of fashion merchandise is its short selling life.

The retailer will generally have to place orders for fashion goods well in advance of the selling season, so that the manufacturers will have time to produce the necessary merchandise. The orders must usually be placed between three and six months before the season begins. The retailer is placed in the difficult position of having to forecast several months in advance what will be the public's preference for fashion goods — something which is notoriously difficult to predict from one week to the next. Furthermore, the retailer has to commit himself to firm orders at this stage, so that he is taking the major part of the risk that the merchandise will not sell. The evaluation and selection of the range of merchandise offered by the manufacturers several months before the selling season begins is the most difficult and interesting part of the fashion buyer's work.

At this initial ordering stage, retailers have to commit between 50 and 80 per cent of their buying budget for the season, and the success of the department will depend heavily on the accuracy of the initial selection, and on the way the remainder of the budget is handled during the selling season itself.

When the selling season begins, the manufacturer will have produced the majority of the pre-season orders. Some will still be in process, and much of his manufacturing capacity may now be taken up producing next season's merchandise, but he is likely to have some flexibility remaining in the total amount of each style he produces, and he may have taken a chance on some styles and produced more than was ordered. These two factors represent the reserve flexibility available to the fashion buyer as the beginning of the season, and both will dwindle very rapidly as the season progresses.

During the first few weeks of the season, the buyer will have the opportunity to see whether the merchandise he has selected is performing as expected, or whether some action should be taken to change the situation. There are a number of possible actions open to him to enable him to maximize the profitability of his department. There are two major considerations at this stage. Firstly, the buyer is interested in making as many sales as possible of his good lines, and the more merchandise he has in stock, the more sales he is likely to make. However, there is a limited time in which he can make these sales; if he is left with a large stock at the end of the selling season, he will have to dispose of the merchandise rapidly, and this means selling it at a low price. The buyer has to balance the likely profit from sales against the probable losses he will have to take from being over-stocked at the end of the season. On this basis, he will have to decide what action to take for each style of merchandise in the department. His possible courses of action are as follows:

1 Do nothing, because the performance so far is up to expecta-
   tions, and the information he has received is inconclusive. The
   actual sales so far this season are neither good enough nor
   bad enough to justify taking drastic action.
2 Reorder the style from the manufacturer. This style has been
   selling particularly well, and he needs to replace the stock sold.
   The chances are that the manufacturer has no extra supply of
   this style, and he may have no extra production capacity to
   make more. In this case the buyer will have to search through
   what merchandise is available to find a style as similar as
   possible to the one he wishes to reorder.
3 Mark down the price of the style to clear it out of the department. In his opinion the style is not performing well, and is
   likely to be over-stocked at the end of the season. The earlier
   it can be marked down, the longer the opportunity it will have
   of selling out, and more space and money will be made available
   for selling more profitable lines.
4 Transfer the stock of this style from the outlets where it is
   selling badly to other outlets where it is selling well. This is a
   fairly unusual situation, but it can happen that a style sells
   well in one location and poorly in another. Excessive transfer-
   ring of stock between locations involves considerable transportation costs, so that the difference in performance has to be
   significant before this kind of action can be justified.

These, then, are the problems facing the fashion buyer. How can
automatic stock-control techniques help him solve them?

There is very little that stock-control theory (at its present stage
of development) can do to help the buyer with his initial evaluation
and selection of merchandise. Automatic forecasting techniques
have been used with considerable success in estimating the total
value of sales made by a fashion department as a whole in the
coming season, so that sales forecasts by department, or by outlet
by department, can be generated by a forecasting system and used
as a guide in allocating the total proportion of the buying budget to
each department in the store. The reason why forecasting techniques
can be used here is that, although the styles in a particular department will change each year, the department itself will continue to
exist. Therefore a valid sales history is available for the total department, which can be used as a basis for forecasting future sales.

The major contribution which can be made in the area of fashion merchandise is in the evaluation of styles during the selling season itself. When the season has begun, the most important factor in the success of the department is the speed of response to the actual sales of the styles being sold. If a style is to be reordered, the earlier this is done the better. If the manufacturer receives a reorder early in the season, he is more likely to have production capacity available to fill the order, and the first retailer to make his reorders is likely to capture the extra stock of good styles and the extra production capacity, so that very little flexibility will remain for his competitors. Furthermore, the longer the extra stock is available in the store, the more chance it will have of selling during the limited season. Likewise, if a style is performing badly, the earlier it is marked down the better. If bad sellers are allowed to remain in the department until the end-of-season sales, they take up display space that could have been allocated to profitable lines, and they tie up inventory money which could have been invested in better merchandise. Also, the earlier a bad seller is marked down, the more time it will have in which to sell out, so that panic markdowns to a very low price at the end of the season can be minimized. If a bad seller is detected very early in the season, it is possible that the manufacturer can be prevented from making the complete order, especially if he can be asked simultaneously to switch the production capacity to a more profitable style using the same materials. All these things can be achieved given a rapid analysis of the early-season performance of styles.

The major difficulty experienced in the evaluation of style performance under present conditions is the very large amount of information to be collected and analysed. For a buyer to analyse all the sales data from every location for every style within his department week by week would be almost impossible. He generally has to depend upon feed-back from the individual department managers in each outlet, and upon sample results from the individual locations he visits or monitors closely. It must also be remembered that the buyer will be spending much of his time in selection and evaluation of the merchandise for the next season at this time, so that he cannot devote his full attention to the problem. It is quite common for the function of controlling merchandise during the season to be taken away from the buyer and given to a merchandise controller.

However, the large volume of information can be analysed by

automatic techniques and electronic computers, so as to give the buyer full information on what has occurred so far in the selling season. Ideally the automatic techniques could select and pre-digest the information, so as to draw the buyer's attention to particular styles in need of action. In this way the retailer would be able to gain the benefit of very rapid analysis and reaction to sales during the season. At its present stage of development stock-control theory can provide a very good guide to the buyer on which merchandise to reorder, which to transfer and which to mark down during the selling season.

The theoretical basis of automatic inventory control of fashion merchandise is fairly simple, and is a logical extension of techniques at present in use in the fashion industry. The first principle involves the way in which sales are calculated and evaluated. Because of the high risk of having dead stock at the end of the short selling season, fashion goods are bought in small quantities. A given style of dress may have five or six different colours and six or seven major sizes. Thus, in order to have a full coverage of items in the style, one would have to buy at least thirty units of a style for each location. In fact it would be more sensible to have several units of the more common sizes and the more fashionable colours, so that it is necessary to buy between fifty and one hundred units to give full size/colour coverage. The fashion retailer has neither the space nor the confidence in the likely sales of a style to buy on this scale for each location. Therefore most fashion styles have a very thin size/colour coverage. When a customer arrives in the store, she will want a particular size, and often a particular colour of merchandise. If there is a small stock of the style, then it is quite likely that she will not find the particular combination she requires in that style. For this reason, the sales of a fashion style are usually proportional to the stock held. Any evaluation of the performance of fashion merchandise has to consider the ratio of sales to stock rather than the sales figure in isolation. This principle is well established in the fashion industry. A theoretical analysis of style profitability comes to a similar conclusion, with another factor added to the evaluation. Assume that the fashion retailer invests a certain amount of money in stock of a particular style. This is the cost of the merchandise bought. From this investment he expects a certain return, which is the profit he makes from selling the style. From these figures, the amount of return on investment can be calculated for a given style.

investment = cost price × number of units in stock = cI

return = (selling price − cost price) × sales = $(r − c)S$

$$\text{return on investment} = \frac{(r − c)S}{cI}$$

which is equal to the sales divided by inventory (the sales to stock ratio) multiplied by the mark-on on cost (the amount of profit for one sale divided by the item cost price). This is the theoretical profitability figure, which I.B.M. call the 'style inventory effectiveness index'.

Given an automatic sales-recording system, this figure can be calculated very rapidly for each style in a department by a computer, and can be used in several different ways in analysing style performance. The most successful method to date has been to divide styles into functional groups, and monitor the profitability of each style within the group against the average group performance. If the performance of a style is significantly different from that of the rest of the group it is selected for action, and the buyer is asked to make a decision on these selected styles. In practice, buyers with this kind of back-up have been able to control their departments very much more profitably in a number of well-controlled experiments. The major advantages have been higher sales, because the average selling ratio of the styles in stock has been maintained at a high level through cutting out unprofitable styles early and obtaining more stock of the good sellers, thus using the inventory space and money more effectively; higher maintained mark-on, because bad sellers were eliminated more effectively and earlier; and a lower average stock level, through producing a rapid turn-over of unprofitable as well as profitable merchandise.

Chapter 10
The Implementation of Automatic Stock Control Systems

The inventory control techniques described in the previous chapters can be used in many different ways in order to lay more or less emphasis on the various objectives which an inventory control system can have. It is therefore essential to define exactly what objectives are to be aimed for, and their relative importance. The two most important purposes of stock control are to increase sales and to reduce stock costs. I think it is fair to say that most accountants, given the responsibility for devising such a system, would lay great emphasis on the desirability of stock reductions. Likewise, a sales manager or chief buyer in this situation would tend to stress the importance of increasing sales at the expense of economic stock levels. Certainly in the wholesale and retail environment, where inventory is such a major portion of the business, decisions which affect the way stock will be used should be the responsibility of the highest management personnel, at least in the initial stages, and decisions made at this stage should have authority from the highest level. The main reason for this is that decisions on the relative importance of these conflicting objectives require a balanced view of the company as a whole rather than a limited departmental view. Furthermore, many promising inventory control schemes have been wrecked on the rock of interdepartmental rivalries or lack of co-operation. This danger can be minimized if the scheme is installed with positive support from the top echelons of management.

What, then, are the major decisions to be taken? Firstly, with a stock-control system of a given power, what emphasis should be placed on increasing sales, and what emphasis on reducing stock? Secondly, how much money should be spent on the inventory control system, how complex does it have to be, and how much reward will the extra complexity provide? Thirdly, what methods of data gathering and processing should be used, relative to the size of the problem and volume of information to be handled and the sophistication of the stock-control techniques? Fourthly, what emphasis should be given to the less easily defined factors such as customer service, providing a steady lead time, etc., and what extra advantages to the customer can be extracted from the basic system, such as early warning of low stock situations, automated billing and better discount structures? Fifthly, and somewhat later in time, where should the system be first installed; is it beginning to achieve its objectives; if not, what alterations should be made; and how fast should it be expanded into the other locations or types of merchandise? The gathering of the basic data for these decisions is the first step in implementing a stock-control system.

In deciding what increase in sales or reduction in stock should be aimed for or expected, the first step is to analyse the present environment to discover what service level is being achieved, and for what average stock costs. The ease or difficulty of carrying out this analysis depends very much on how much basic information is available, and how many different items of merchandise have to be considered. If records of stock and sales are readily available, it is relatively easy to discover the average stock value of the merchandise. It is generally too costly and time-consuming to analyse every item in every location. Results are therefore generally drawn from a sample of the stock-keeping units in the organization. This should preferably be a random sample, and the size of the sample chosen can be determined by a statistician from the accuracy required, the number of stock-keeping units in the whole inventory, and the amount of effort available to make the analysis. Once the average stock level of the sample has been determined, the service level *of the same sample* should be analysed. If records of stock-outs or back-orders are readily available and reliable, there is very little problem in calculating the service level of the sample as sales divided by sales plus back-orders. Otherwise, it is possible to deduce the service level from the sales and from a sampling study of the stock-out situation. By looking at the inventory of the items in the sample at regular intervals over a period of perhaps three months, the stock-out frequency for each item in the sample can be approximately determined. If this stock-out frequency is converted to a frequency per year, and multiplied by the average annual sales for each item separately, and the result accumulated, an approximate figure for lost sales or back-orders per annum can be determined for the sample. The service level can then be calculated as sales divided by sales plus back-orders (or sales plus lost sales) as before. If no data are available initially, then the sampling study for the items involved must also determine approximate figures for sales rate and average stock level.

By applying the order point and order quantity formulae to the sales patterns of the items in the sample, a range of possible strategies can be examined, with different combinations of stock level and service level (and hence sales). An example would perhaps be of use at this point. A sample was taken of the items in a wholesale inventory. Five hundred items were chosen at random from the total range of ten thousand. The average stock value of these items was £30,000, and their average service level was found to be 94 per cent. Approximate calculations showed that there was a range of possible stock levels and service levels from which the following points were chosen:

Stock value	Service level (per cent)
£20,000	94
£25,000	97
£30,000	98·5
£37,000	99
£50,000	99·5

Based on an inventory carrying cost of 30 per cent, average annual sales of the sample of £300,000, the proportion of back-orders which were estimated to cause lost sales or serious customer dissatisfaction, and on the ordering work-load considered to be within the capabilities of the existing staff, the management took the view that a service level of 98·5 per cent with no change in average stock level would be the optimum policy. The expected increase in sales over the whole inventory was £200,000 per annum, which more than justified the proposed changes in inventory procedure.

To answer the second question, how costly and complex the inventory control system should be, further analyses should be carried out on the sampled items, in order to determine what improvements in service level or stock level would be produced by more sophisticated techniques, and what extra cost would be involved in the use of such techniques. The major alternatives at this point are whether the system should be based on an electronic computer, or whether a manual system could produce satisfactory results at less cost. This decision can be influenced by many factors; in particular, if the use of a computer is considered, what other benefits could be derived from such a machine when it is not carrying out stock-control calculations. The most important factor is probably the volume of work to be handled. If a company has to control a large number of separate items in many locations, and the stock situation must be reviewed frequently, then a large work-load is involved, and a computerized solution is likely to be preferable. If fewer stock-keeping units are involved, then the problem may be handled adequately by clerical personnel. Retail stores, for example, which typically sell tens or hundreds of thousands of different items through many different outlets, and whose stock needs frequent review, will probably benefit most from the use of computers for stock control. Wholesalers also need to control tens of thousands of items in multiple warehouses, and are good candidates for this kind of operation. Fashion houses, which need very rapid response to changes in demand, and consequently very frequent review and analysis of stock, are also in a high work-load situation. In manufacturing companies, the case for computerization of inventories may be more doubtful from the point of view of work-load, as the number of different products and locations to be controlled becomes smaller. However, such companies are more likely to be using computers for other purposes, and can often gain great advantages from integrating stock control with their other procedures on a computer. Finished goods and raw-material inventories are a useful input and output to an automatic production scheduling system, and products involving complex assemblies from manufactured and acquired parts often require a sophisticated stock-control system to keep track of when and where particular parts are required, and to maintain the correct stock levels of a large number of basic parts.

The major difference between an automated operation and clerical control is the amount of free play for initiative. Although a clerk may be following fixed reordering techniques, the process is far less automatic. A computer will stick rigidly to the stock-control rules given to it, and should refer exceptional cases to the stock controller, whereas it is often said that a company using clerical control has as many inventory policies as it has stock-clerks; there is a considerable problem in communicating the policy decisions on stock management down to lower levels. On the other hand, if the type of merchandise to be controlled demands frequent exercise of initiative, and the stock-control rules are inadequate, then a computer will find it difficult to function effectively. The remainder of this chapter is biased towards implementation by means of a computer, as this is a more complex subject, probably less familiar to the average stock controller. Procedures for installing a more efficient manual operation are similar but more simple.

An automatic stock-control system should be installed gradually, starting with a small range of merchandise in one location, and gradually expanding this to more locations and to a wider range of merchandise. This procedure has many advantages, the most obvious of which is that the system can be tried out in practice on a small enough volume of items to permit complete verification of each order produced; it is almost certain that there will be errors and inadequacies in the system at the initial stages, where the stock-control rules do not cover certain practical situations in the particular company involved. Once the necessary amendments have been made, the system can be applied more widely. There may be considerable resistance to overcome from the buying staff, who are likely to be reluctant to delegate the more mechanical parts of their job to automatic procedures. It is often advisable to initiate the experiment in the department controlled by a particularly receptive buyer, who is anxious to take advantage of more advanced methods. In this way, reports of the success of the first experiment should encourage the remainder of the staff to accept the system themselves. Also, there is normally a considerable amount of data gathering and preparation required in order to initiate the system on a certain number of items. If this load of data collection can be spread over a long period, giving priority to those groups of merchandise and locations scheduled for early implementation, the operation should be carried out with a smoother work-load, and allow the staff involved to learn from any errors or inadequacies which appear in the data collection for the first few merchandise groups.

Once it is decided what the major objectives of the system are, and where it will first be installed, it is very important to prepare for the measurement of the effect of the system. It is essential to know whether or not the broad objectives are being achieved, missed or exceeded, and this implies keeping records of average stock, service level, sales, number of orders placed, cost of clerical labour, and so on both before and after the system has begun to operate. A monthly summary of the stock and service position and other costs should be monitored by the project manager (who should report directly to top management, as explained previously), so that the expected results can be proved and the experience gained applied to the probable savings when the system has spread to the entire inventory. Some caution should be exercised when reviewing the first few months of operation, as both stock levels and service levels are likely to be higher than planned for some time. The reason for this is that the system will attempt to rebalance the inventory by ordering more merchandise for those items it considers to be under-stocked, and by allowing the stock to run down on those items it considers to be over-stocked. However, the replenishment of under-stocked items is likely to be more rapid than the selling off of over-stocks, so that the net effect will be a temporary increase in stock. If the initial inventory was very out of balance, very large increases in stock can occur during the first two or three months. Computer simulations of the likely behaviour of the stock during the transition period between the old and new systems can be of great value in predicting these effects.

If the decision is made to use computers to control stock, then there are a large number of procedures to be designed and problems to be solved. The initial setting-up of the operation may be time-consuming and expensive, although it is to be hoped that this will be more than justified by the savings made when the system becomes operational. The first decision to be made is the method of presentation of the basic information to the computer. In some way the sales and receipts of merchandise must be presented in a machine-readable form, so that the sales, receipts and stock balance can be maintained by the computer. There are two ways in which this can be done. One method is to record each sale (or issue) as it occurs, and generate some machine-readable document which specifies what article was sold from what location in what quantity—in other words, sales recording. The second alternative is to make a regular count of the amount of stock of each item remaining, so that a document is generated, say every month, for each item in each location, which specifies which article was counted, and how much stock of that article was available. In both cases the receipts of merchandise into the store must also be recorded. The three items to be recorded—receipts, sales and stock balance—can be calculated by a machine provided that any two of them are specified.

There are many methods of producing machine-readable documents to record stock or sales, ranging from systems which involve the typing of information from documents on to punched cards, through the attachment of special tags to each article as it is received in the store, to the direct reading of handwritten figures by a computer. Whatever method is used, the recording of stock movements will often be one of the major costs involved in the system.

The decision as to whether stock or sales should be recorded depends heavily on the speed of movement, and the unit value of the merchandise in question. If the merchandise is high-value, sales recording is likely to be more attractive; if the merchandise is fast-moving, stock recording is likely to be preferable. Any individual case can be costed out fairly easily, from the number of movements per year, the frequency of stock counting required and the relative costs of stock counting and sales recording. The direct recording of sales or issues often appears to be more attractive at first sight. The necessary recording can be added to the normal sales or issuing procedure with little difficulty, especially if some kind of detachable record is used. However, receipts procedures are complicated by the necessity to attach tags to the goods as they arrive, which offers another area in which gross errors can be made. An advantage of stock counting, although it is probably intrinsically less accurate, is that it is largely self-correcting: if too low a figure is recorded this month, it is likely that a more correct figure will occur next month, and that the high sales calculated in error this month will be compensated for by artificially low sales next month. If errors are extreme they can be detected by the fact that negative sales will be calculated for the item in question, which should always produce a query from the computer. Furthermore, stock counting automatically records pilferage, which tends to persist as a discrepancy in sales-recording systems. In stock-recording systems the timing of receipts often becomes a problem. If, for example, the computer has recorded last month's stock as 50 units, and this month's stock as 30 units, together with a receipt of 20 units, it is difficult to tell whether sales during last month were 20 or 40 unless it is certain that the merchandise received was in its correct location by the time the stock count was made. This disadvantage applies far less strongly to the sales-recording system, which knows that the stock is either there now or will be very soon. Whichever method is used, accuracy in recording basic data will be a significant problem.

In general, the automatic systems described in this book will work reasonably well with 95 per cent or more accuracy of data capture, and it is usually possible to attain this level of accuracy in practice without prohibitively expensive checking procedures.

Once a sales- or stock-recording system has been designed, it will probably be necessary to design another information-gathering system in order to obtain the basic data to begin operations. In particular, it is necessary to obtain past sales history values on which the initial computer sales forecasts can be based. If it is difficult to extract information from existing sales records (and it is usually next to impossible), this may present considerable problems. One unattractive solution is to allow the sales-recording system to build up enough history to operate from; but companies are seldom willing to wait for two years of sales recording before any significant benefit is extracted from inventory control. However, most modern forecasting systems can be successfully initiated from estimates of the sales level and seasonal patterns of the items, or by being directed to take the sales history of a similar item as the basis for forecasting a new item, so that this step can where necessary be considerably simplified. When actual history is not made available to the system for a large proportion of the items, there may be a considerable time-lag before the *full* benefits of automatic control are realized, depending on the accuracy of the initial estimates and the lead times and usages of the individual items.

Other basic data to be obtained are usually much simpler to come by. Item lead times and prices, and the related supplier discount structure, must be recorded, and it is often valuable to take the opportunity to write to all suppliers to have them quote lead times and discounts. Lead times may become more reliable if the supplier knows that an automated system will be checking on the lead times produced, and it is quite common for buying departments to discover several new discount opportunities of which they were previously unaware. Once basic data on prices and sales rates are available, several interesting analyses can be made to determine which lines contribute most to company turnover and profit, and which least. Low-usage items can be selected for discontinuation, and some items left out of the stock-control system altogether, as the cost of controlling them would outweigh the advantage gained; instead, a simple rule-of-thumb system can be installed for such items.

Several major parameters will have to be decided at an early stage; in particular the frequency of stock review will affect both the running cost and the performance of the system. These can often be decided by simulation of the system, using a computer to evaluate the effect of alternative policies on the stock and service levels. Techniques of simulation of stock-control systems are quite advanced, and valuable predictions of the effect of different service levels, inventory levels, ordering rules, forecast and review intervals and so on can be obtained by these methods at quite a low cost without having to experiment in practice using 'live' merchandise.

Once these basic data have been obtained, and the preliminary analyses and decisions made, the system can be initiated. At this point, the success of the system depends very much upon the closeness of control and amount of support given to the project manager, whose major objectives must be to tailor the system to any requirements which appear during the run-in period, to satisfy his management that sufficiently promising results are being achieved, and to win the confidence of the buying staff.

Automatic stock-control systems of any complexity are still quite rare anywhere, and the majority of experience comes from wholesale organizations in the U.S.A. In Europe there have been several successful installations of automatic systems, notably in Sweden. Retail companies in this country and the U.S.A. have recently begun to use automatic systems, and have experienced considerable success to date. The results of this kind of operation vary according to the efficiency or otherwise of the previous manual systems, and according to whether the company was previously running on a high stock level or a low service level. In several cases stock has been reduced by as much as 40 per cent, the usual figure being between 20 and 30 per cent, without any deterioration in service level; in other cases, service levels have been increased by up to 50 per cent without any corresponding increase in stock. The most common result is an increase in service together with a reduction in stock. It has been convincingly demonstrated that the advantages of an automatic stock-control system will usually repay handsomely the initial investment in setting up such a system.

Bibliography

Inventory Control

R. G. BROWN, *Statistical Forecasting for Inventory Control*, McGraw-Hill, 1959.

J. W. FORRESTER, *Industrial Dynamics*, Massachusetts Institute of Technology, 1961

H. G. HADLEY & T. M. WHITIN, *Analysis of Inventory Systems*, Prentice-Hall, 1963.

C. C. HOLT *et al.*, *Planning Production, Inventories and Work Force*, Prentice-Hall, 1960.

J. F. MAGEE & D. M. BOODMAN, *Production Planning and Inventory Control*, McGraw-Hill, 1967.

P. M. MORSE, *Queues, Inventories and Maintenance*, Wiley, 1958.

W. E. WELCH, *Scientific Inventory Control*, Management Publishing Co., 1956.

T. M. WHITIN, *Theory of Inventory Management*, Princeton University Press, 1953.

Forecasting

R. G. BROWN, *Smoothing, Forecasting and Prediction of Discrete Time Series*, Prentice-Hall, 1962.

E. H. MACNIECE, *Production Forecasting, Planning and Control*, Wiley, 1961.

D. W. TRIGG, 'Monitoring forecasting systems', *Operational Research Quarterly*, vol. xv, 1964, pp. 271–4.

D. W. TRIGG & A. G. LEACH, 'Exponential smoothing with an adaptive response rate', *Operational Research Quarterly*, vol. xviii, 1967, pp. 53–59.

Index